D0899755

Using STEM to Investigate Issues in Food Production

Authors: Barbara R. Sandall, Ed.D., and Abha Singh, Ph.D.

Consultants: Schrylet Cameron and Suzanne Myers

Editors and Proofreader: Mary Dieterich, Sarah M. Anderson, and Margaret Brown

COPYRIGHT © 2011 Mark Twain Media, Inc.

ISBN 978-1-58037-579-5

Printing No. CD-404142

Mark Twain Media, Inc., Publishers
Distributed by Carson-Dellosa Publishing LLC

Visit us at www.carsondellosa.com

Table of Contents

Introduction to *Using STEM to Investigate Issues in Food Production* iii

    Introduction to the Series iii

    Science, Technology, and Society iii

    Technological Design Process iv

    Mathematical Problem Solving v

    Introduction to Food Production v

Chapter One: Food Production Issues 1

Chapter Two: Biologically Productive Land & Water 16

Chapter Three: Food Systems, Chains, & Webs 34

Chapter Four: Food and Energy 45

Chapter Five: Farming 55

Chapter Six: Hydroponics 68

Chapter Seven: Food Processing & Preservation 83

Chapter Eight: STEM Design Challenge 94

APPENDICES

    Science Inquiry Skills Assessment 102

    Assessment of Technological Design 104

    Science Process Skills 105

    National Science Education Standards (NSES) 106

    Principles and Standards for School Mathematics (NCTM) 111

    International Standards for Technological Literacy (ITEA) 113

    Assessment Answer Keys 117

    References 118

Introduction to *Using STEM to Investigate Issues in Food Production*

Introduction to the Series

The *STEMs of Learning: Science, Technology, Engineering, and Mathematics* is an initiative designed to get students interested in these career fields. In 2009, the National Academy of Engineering (NAE) and the National Research Council (NRC) reported that there is a lack of focus on the science, technology, engineering, and mathematics (STEM) subjects in K–12 schools. This creates concerns about the competitiveness of the United States in the global market and the development of a workforce with the knowledge and skills needed to address technical and technological issues. The focus of many current STEM education programs is on mathematics and science and not on engineering and technology. This series was developed to encourage students to become a part of the solution and increase interest in the STEM areas. The series introduces students to the use of STEM skills to solve problems. It is our hope that through these investigations students will become interested in the STEM areas of study.

The *Using STEM to Investigate Series* provides fun and meaningful integrated activities that cultivate an interest in topics in the STEM fields of science, technology, engineering, and mathematics and encourages students to explore careers in these fields. The series introduces students to the following topics: Issues in Alternative Energy, Issues in Food Production, and Issues in Managing Waste using science, mathematics, engineering, and technological design as a means for problem solving and scientific inquiry. Students actively engage in solving real-world problems using scientific inquiry, content knowl-

edge, and technological design. All of the activities are aligned with the National Science Education Standards (NSES), the National Council of Teachers of Mathematics (NCTM) Standards, and the International Technology Education Association (ITEA) Standards for Technological Literacy. For correlations to state, national, and Canadian provincial standards, visit www.carsondellosa.com.

The series is written for classroom teachers, parents, families, and students. The books in this series can be used as a full unit of study or as individual lessons to supplement existing curriculum programs or textbooks. Activities are designed to be pedagogically sound, hands-on minds-on activities that support the national standards. Parents and students can use this series as an enhancement to what is done in the classroom or as a tutorial at home. The procedures and content background are clearly explained in the introduction and within the individual activities. Materials used are commonly found in classrooms and homes or can be ordered from science supply sources.

Science, Technology, and Society

Science, technology, and society are very closely related. Science and technology have impacted personal and community health, population growth, natural resources, and environmental quality. It is important for students to understand the interrelationship of science, technology, and society because

Introduction to *Using STEM to Investigate Issues in Food Production* (cont.)

these factors impact their daily lives all over the world. Science advances new technology, and using new technology increases scientific knowledge.

Science and technology are pursued for different reasons. Science inquiry is driven by the desire to understand the natural world. Technology is driven by the need to solve problems and meet human needs. Technology usually has more of a direct effect on society. For example, the creation of the telephone, computers, and the Internet have had a large impact on the way our society communicates. Science and technology have also impacted the diagnoses and treatment of diseases that have increased the longevity of the human race. Science and technology have created more comfortable places for us to live in most areas of the world. However, science and technology have also had a negative impact on our environment. As a new technology that we need or want is developed, the impact on the environment must be closely examined.

The National Science Education Standards (NSES) unifying concepts and science processes skills integrate the areas of science, technology, engineering, and mathematics (STEM). The unifying concepts include systems, order, and organization; evidence, models, and explanations; change, constancy, and measurement; evolution and equilibrium; and form and function. The processes of inquiry are skills used in all content areas and in our everyday lives to investigate and solve problems. These science process skills include the basic skills of classifying, observing, measuring, inferring, communicating, predicting, manipulating materials, replicating, using numbers, developing vocabulary, questioning, and using cues. The integrated science process skills include creating models, formulating a hypothesis, generalizing, identifying and controlling variables, defining operationally, recording and interpreting data, making decisions, and experimenting. See the Appendix for a list of skills and definitions.

Technological Design Process

The NSES recommend that students have abilities and understandings of technological design and about science and technology. The NSES Science and Technology Content Standard E states that the technological design process includes identifying a problem or design opportunity; proposing designs and possible solutions; implementing the solution; evaluating the solution and its consequences; and communicating the problem, processes, and solution. Creativity, imagination, and a good content background are necessary in working in science and engineering. The process is a continuous cycle.

The International Technology Education Association (ITEA) Standards for Technological Literacy also suggest that students develop abilities for a technological world that include applying the design process to solve a problem, using and maintaining technological products, and assessing the impact of the products on the environment and society. Students should have an understanding of the attributes of design and engineering design and the role of troubleshooting, research and development, inventions and innovations, and experimentation in problem solving. The design process includes identifying and collecting information about everyday problems that can be solved by technology. It also includes generating ideas and requirements for solving the problems. See the Appendix for a list of skills and definitions.

Introduction to *Using STEM to Investigate Issues in Food Production* (cont.)

Mathematical Problem Solving

The National Council of Teachers of Mathematics (NCTM) recommends that students develop abilities to use problem-solving skills, formulate problems, develop and apply a variety of strategies to solve problems, verify and interpret results, and generalize solutions and strategies to new problems. Students also need to be able to communicate with models, orally, in writing, and with pictures and graphs; reflect and clarify their own thinking; use the skills of reading, listening, and observing to interpret and evaluate ideas; and be able to make conjectures and convincing arguments. Students should be able to recognize and apply reasoning processes, make and evaluate arguments, validate their own thinking, and use the power of reasoning to solve problems. All of these skills are related to science and technology, as well as mathematics. See the Appendix for a list of skills and definitions.

Introduction to Food Production

Food production in the world has reached a crisis level. The population of the world is growing, and food production, processing, preservation, and distribution are not keeping up with the population growth. The impact of food production on the health and welfare of society and the environment needs to be investigated to resolve this crisis. The cause of this food crisis is greatly debated. Agricultural engineers and scientists are working to solve the problems related to how to produce, preserve, process, and distribute food to all people in a safe and effective way with little negative impact on the environment.

There are two sides to the food production issue. One side encourages local food and sustainability. The other side believes that food production should be as efficient and as productive as possible. Food prices should be kept low and adequate reserves for bad crop years should be maintained. U.S. farmers are trying to balance sustainable farm practices with higher productivity.

Eric Holt-Gimenéz suggests the root cause of the food crisis is the global food system. The global food system is the sum of all global interactions among food, agriculture, water, energy, soil, and humans that comprise our food system. The global food system is vulnerable to the economic and environmental impact of international grain traders, corporations (seed, chemical, and fertilizer processors), and global market chains. In order to resolve the food crisis, the food system needs to be fixed. Some areas of concern include: government support of domestic food production and stabilizing fair prices to farmers, workers, and consumers; the halt of agrofuel expansion and the re-regulatation of the financial sector investment in food commodities; the return to small family farms and locally based approaches to food production and food system management; and finally, creating a social change in the way food is managed. This means reducing the political influence of large corporations and strengthening antitrust laws and enforcement of these laws.

Introduction to *Using STEM to Investigate Issues in Food Production* (cont.)

Some believe the only way to feed a growing population is by genetically modified crops and the use of chemical pesticides and fertilizers. However, newer scientific studies recommend sustainable farming as a better way. The U.S. Working Group on the Food Crisis report *Can Sustainable Agriculture Feed the World?* recommends that an investment should be made in sustainable agriculture. Sustainable agriculture or agroecology (the science of sustainable agriculture) combines scientific methods with local farming knowledge to create diverse and productive food production systems without relying on expensive seeds and chemicals. International assessments done by the International Assessment of Agricultural Knowledge, Science and Technology for Development in 2008 indicated that conventional industrial agriculture degrades soils and other natural resources and threatens water, energy resources, and the global climate. A United Nations Environment Program confirmed their findings. Both studies encourage the development of sustainable food production.

The following trends are hot topics in food production. Organic farming doubled from 2000 to 2007. Organic farming typically avoids the use of chemical and genetically modified organisms. It relies on ecological processes rather than chemical fertilizers, pesticides, and herbicides. Genetically modified crops were produced on 114.3 million hectares or 282.3 million acres in 2007. Genetically modified crops have been modified through genetic engineering, which eliminates, alters, or introduces new genetic elements, including from one unrelated species to another. In 2008, grain production rose to 2.287 billion tons. From 1993 to 2008, the amount of land used for grain has remained steady at 700 million hectares, but crop yields are up 146% over the last 46 years. All stages of the food system—seeds, farming, processing, preserving—are being consolidated into a few corporate firms. In 2009, 1.02 billion people

in the world were undernourished or suffered from chronic hunger, which is an increase of 12% since 2008. One in six people in the world suffer from undernourishment. Undernourishment means people are receiving less than 1,800 kilocalories (kcal) a day compared to the 3,400 kcal per day in the United States, Canada, and Europe. In 2009, the world population went over 6.8 billion. It is projected the population will be 9.4 billion by 2050. Meat production increased to 280 million tons in 2008 and has doubled since the mid 1970s, with more than half of the meat and dairy products being produced in developing nations. Fish production—wild and farmed in aquaculture—increased to 158 million tons in 2008. Aquaculture is the most rapidly growing area in food production. In 2007, 80% of fish stocks were fully used or overused.

All of the current trends in food production require an examination of the overall world food system from seed to table. All of these reports recommend developing a sustainable food production system. This book on food production examines the issues of producing food for a growing population while trying not to have a negative impact on consumers or the environment.

Chapter One: Food Production Issues

Teacher Information

Topic: Issues in food production

Standards:
NSES – Unifying Concepts and Processes
Systems, Order, and Organization
Form and Function

NSES – Content
NSES A: Science as Inquiry
NSES B: Physical Science
NSES C: Life Science
NSES D: Earth and Space
NSES E: Science and Technology
NSES F: Personal and Social Perspectives
NSES G: Science as a Human Endeavor

NCTM:
Problem Solving
Communication
Reasoning
Mathematical Connections
Probability

ITEA:
Nature of Technology
Technology and Society
Technological World

Concepts:
Food production
Issues in food production, i.e., need for production of food; sustainable development; policies; organic gardening; green food production; food processing; food distribution; amount of land and water resources that are productive; population growth; livestock production; transportation of food; impact on the environment; chemical herbicides, pesticides, and fertilizers; etc.

Objectives:
Students will be able to…
- Examine their own beliefs and values to make decisions related to food production.
- Debate the issues, respecting the rights of others to maintain different rights and values.
- Evaluate possible solutions to food production issues.
- Explain what needs to be considered when making decisions about managing food production.

Activity – Food Production Issue Discussion Sheets (p. 6–12)

Materials:
Issue Discussion Sheets

TEACHER NOTE: The major purpose of this activity is to help students learn about the issues involved in food production. Prior to starting, the teacher should discuss the rules for discussion (i.e., all students have the right to their own opinions, they will listen to and respect each other's ideas, etc.). Reproduce the number of sets of sheets needed for groups of four students. Each group should have a set.

Chapter One: Food Production Issues

Student Information

Topic: Issues in food production

Concepts:

Food production
Issues in food production, i.e., need for production of food; sustainable development; policies; organic gardening; green food production; food processing; food distribution; amount of land and water resources that are productive; population growth; livestock production; transportation of food; impact on the environment; chemical herbicides, pesticides, and fertilizers; etc.

Objectives:

Students will be able to…

• Examine their own beliefs and values to make decisions related to food production.
• Debate the issues, respecting the rights of others to maintain different rights and values.
• Evaluate possible solutions to food production issues.
• Explain what needs to be considered when making decisions about managing food production.

Content Background:

Over 6.8 billion people live on Earth, with some 7 million people being born every month. By 2012, over 7 billion people will be sharing the same land, water, and air. It is difficult for the planet to support this many people, and as a result, over 925 million people live in chronic hunger, which means that they never get enough food to eat.

Food scientists struggle to increase the amount of food produced. There are two sides to the food production issue. One side believes that every food production system should be as efficient and as productive as possible. It should keep the food prices low and maintain adequate reserves for bad crop years. Some believe the only way to feed a growing population is with genetically modified crops that produce more grain while using chemical pesticides and fertilizers to increase output. Some people believe giving artificial growth hormones and antibiotics to animals will produce more and better meat.

The other side of the food production debate encourages local food and sustainability. Newer scientific studies recommend sustainable farming as a better way. The U.S. Working Group on the Food Crisis report *Can Sustainable Agriculture Feed the World?* recommends that an investment should be made in sustainable agriculture.

Sustainable agriculture or **agroecology** (the science of sustainable agriculture) combines scientific methods with local farming knowledge to create diverse and productive food production systems without relying on expensive seeds and chemicals. Modern agriculture, using current science, technology, and engineering, has allowed more food to be grown and more fresh foods distributed all over the world. However, the current methods used in commercial agriculture are not a sustainable system.

International assessments done by the International Assessment of Agricultural Knowledge, Science and Technology for Development (IAASTD) in 2008 indicated that conventional

Chapter One: Food Production Issues

Student Information

industrial agriculture degrades soils and other natural resources and threatens water, energy resources, and the global climate. A United Nations Environment Program confirmed their findings. Both studies encourage the development of sustainable food production.

Agricultural engineers identify, investigate, and solve problems related to food and livestock production. Issues related to food production include land and water use; kinds of farming; food distribution; food processing; food safety and preservation; politics and money; a growing population; and food production sustainability.

U.S. farmers are trying to balance sustainable farm practices with higher productivity. Those involved in U.S. crop production have given increased attention to the impact of farming on the environment due to new technology, chemicals, and seed development. Kinds of farming practices such as organic, chemical, crop rotation, small farms, and industrialized farms are all major issues in food production.

The amount of usable land and water on Earth is very small. Earth has a surface area of 51 billion hectares (2.47 acres in one hectare). This is the amount of land that provides food, water, and other resources. If you look at a globe, 28% of the surface is land and the other 72% is water. Of the

28% that is land, 19% is biologically productive; the other 9% is only marginally productive or unproductive.

Land is **biologically productive** if it is fertile enough to support agriculture, forests, or animal life. The marginally productive or unproductive land includes pavement, land covered by ice, land that has no water, or land that has unsuitable soil conditions for plant growth.

Of the 72% of Earth's surface lakes and oceans, only 4% is biologically productive for human use. The other 68% is marginally productive or unproductive water. The productivity may be reduced by destruction of coral reefs, oil spills, overfishing, and shoreline development.

Of the 51 billion hectares of surface area including land and water, only about 23% is biologically productive. This is the only area we have to produce our food, materials, and energy, and to absorb our wastes. We also share this area with 10 million other species.

Recent changes in global weather patterns have brought new challenges to food production. Desertification is one challenge. **Desertification** is the erosion of formerly productive land into deserts. The most famous example of desertification in the United States was the Dust Bowl in the 1930s. Due to poor farming techniques and a long drought, much of the land in Kansas, Oklahoma, and Texas literally blew away. Today, desertification is causing the Sahara desert to expand south across Africa at a rate of 48 km per year. This land goes from being biologically productive to unproductive.

When more land is cleared for farming by removing trees and bushes, the topsoil blows or washes away, causing a need for more chemicals to be added to add necessary nutrients. If land is used over and over for the same crops, all of the nutrients in the soil disappear. One way to avoid this is by adding chemical fertilizers. However,

Chapter One: Food Production Issues

Student Information

chemical fertilizers, pesticides, and herbicides are getting into our lakes, streams, rivers, and other water resources from groundwater contamination around fields and in the runoff from fields.

A **food system** includes all of the steps in food production from farm to table. The food is grown, shipped, processed, shipped again to markets, purchased in stores, transported home by consumers, and eaten. The energy needed includes not just the energy related to growing the food but also for transportation, processing, preserving, planting, and harvesting.

More food is needed to support the increasing population of the world. Some of the solutions to this food shortage are to use more land, add either organic or chemical fertilizers to marginally productive land to enrich the soil, use chemical herbicides and pesticides to increase crop production, and use genetically engineered crops. Small local farms are being replaced by large corporate farms in an effort to produce more food.

To meet the meat needs required by so many people, large livestock confinements are used to produce more meat. In these lots, livestock are sometimes given antibiotics to reduce the chances of infections and hormones to increase growth or milk production. There is some evidence now that these antibiotics and hormones are getting into the human food supply.

Bringing in food from other countries creates new problems. Farmers in other countries may not use the same standards that the United States requires. For example, Brazil uses chemicals that are banned in the U.S. and the European Union because they are harmful to the environment and humans.

Some believe that returning to local organic farms is the best way to get the best foods to the people and support local economies. Organic farming minimizes the use of synthetic fertilizers and pesticides, which reduces agricultural pollu-

tion and reduces the amount of chemicals consumers ingest. Organic farming also uses less fossil fuels and more locally available resources, making it better for the planet. Organic farming doesn't use genetically modified crops, but instead uses local varieties.

One possible solution to the food production problem is the use of hydroponics. **Hydroponics** refers to plants growing without any kind of soil. Plants can grow in other mediums. Some of these mediums include water with nutritional substances added, husks of coconuts, gravel, or mineral wool.

Soil contains nutrients that plants need to grow and provides support to the roots and plant. When it rains, these nutrients are dissolved in water and carried to the plant through the roots. The type of soil and the amount of nutrients in the soil determine how much of the nutrients the plants can absorb and how well it grows.

In hydroponics, nutrients can be dissolved in water and directly absorbed into the roots. The amount of nutrients can be formulated so that the plant can always take in exactly the nutrients that it needs to grow.

Food preservation and processing are an important part of food production. **Food processing and preservation** means the processes by

Chapter One: Food Production Issues

Student Information

which raw food is made suitable for cooking, eating, storing, marketing, and extending their shelf life. In areas where crops cannot be grown year around, there has to be some way to store food to use during the winter months when food cannot be grown.

Historically, fish and meats were dried or salted to preserve them. Louis Pasteur developed the pasteurization process for wine and milk, which killed the organisms that caused foods to spoil. In the 19th and 20th centuries, food preservation was done by heating and sealing foods in jars or cans and by freezing foods to keep them from spoiling.

Food distribution is one of the major issues in food production. **Food distribution** includes local and regional food systems, food miles, energy costs, transportation, oil, etc. One problem in the distribution of food is that not all crops can be grown in all areas, so the only food available in an area are the foods that can be grown in that area. For example, oranges cannot be grown in colder climates.

Since not all food is grown locally, some food is transported from other parts of the world. Ways of preserving food for extended periods of time and carrying it through different temperatures needed to be developed. One way to preserve the food longer and make it easier to transport is by processing the food before it is shipped. Food processing can be done by heating, freezing, pasteurizing, and adding chemical preservatives.

The processing and preservation of foods helps improve food safety. However, it creates other problems in the food system and for the environment. It requires more natural resources such as water, fossil fuels, and land. Packaging and processing food creates more problems with waste management. These packaging materials break down slowly, and the chemicals from these packages and preservation processes can become highly concentrated in our water, air, and soil.

A **sustainable food system** protects or enhances biodiversity, enriches soil, and protects water quality. If the natural systems that provide humans with oxygen, soil, the absorption of carbon dioxide, clean water, and biodiversity are destroyed, the earth will not support life. A sustainable food system avoids using man-made chemicals that stay in the environment longer than a few days.

Man-made substances and chemicals are not easily broken down by natural Earth cycles. They sometimes accumulate in the environment and damage the air, water, and soil. A sustainable food system should not use a lot of plastic packaging, which comes from fossil fuels, or it should develop a way to recycle all packaging.

A sustainable food system must feed all people. It should not feed one community at the expense of others. Resources should be distributed more evenly to all people. Currently, some groups of people around the world are starving while other groups of people are becoming obese because of an overabundance of food. A sustainable food system should use resources efficiently and recycle or reuse wastes.

This book will explore how to develop a sustainable food system to feed the growing population of the world.

Name: _____   Date: _____

Chapter One: Food Production Issues

Student Activity

Activity – Issues in Food Production

Materials:

  Issue Discussion Sheets

Challenge Question: What are some of the issues related to food production?

Procedure:

1. Divide the class into groups of four and give each group a set of issue discussion sheets.
2. One person in the group takes an issue sheet, reads it to the group, and explains the decision they have chosen and why they have made that decision.
3. The other members of the group then share whether they agree or disagree and why they agree or disagree.
4. This continues until all of the issues are discussed in the small groups.

Challenge:

On your own paper, develop a food system that solves some of the problems identified in this activity.

Name: _____   Date: _____

Chapter One: Food Production Issues

Food Production Issue Discussion Sheets

- -

Issue 1 – Farming

Modern industrial agricultural practices are economically productive but are not sustainable. Some think the practices used by industrial agriculture threaten the biological systems necessary for life. These practices have caused topsoil erosion, loss of fertility, arable land losses, and losses to insect pests that become immune to the widely used pesticides.

More food is needed. Possible solutions include using more land; add either organic or chemical fertilizers, herbicides, and pesticides to marginally productive land; and use genetically engineered seeds.

To solve the meat shortage, large livestock confinements are used to quickly produce more meat. Some livestock are given antibiotics to reduce the chances of infections and hormones to increase growth or milk production. There is some evidence now that these antibiotics and hormones are getting into the human food supply.

Some believe that returning to local organic farms is the best way to get the best foods to the people and support local economies.

Question: There is a shortage of food in the world. What should be done?

a. Clear more trees from land for farming.

b. Use a local approach to food production, and raise the food close to where it will be consumed.

c. Reduce the need for antibiotics by allowing livestock to be outside in fields where they can get fresh air and exercise.

d. Try to find a balance of using some chemicals, genetic engineering, and organic farming.

e. Do something else. Explain.

Name: _____   Date: _____

Chapter One: Food Production Issues

Food Production Issue Discussion Sheets

— —

Issue 2 – Environmental Impact of Farming

When more land is cleared for farming by removing trees and bushes, the topsoil blows or washes away, causing a need for more chemicals to be added to provide the necessary nutrients. If land is used over and over for the same crops, all of the nutrients in the soil disappear. One way to avoid this is by adding chemical fertilizers. However, chemical fertilizers, pesticides, and herbicides are getting into our lakes, streams, rivers, and other water resources from groundwater contamination around fields and in the runoff from fields.

U.S. farmers are trying to balance sustainable farm practices with higher productivity. Those involved in U.S. crop production have given increased attention to the impact of farming on the environment due to new technology, chemicals, and seed development.

Bringing in food from other countries creates new problems. Farmers in other countries may not use the same standards to control the impact of farming on the environment and in the food supply. For example, Brazil uses chemicals that were banned in the U.S. and European Union because they are harmful to the environment and humans.

Question: There is a shortage of food in the world. What should be done?

a. Use chemicals, genetic engineering, clear more trees from land for farming, and anything else that would produce more food, even though it may have a negative impact on humans and the environment.

b. Use a local approach to food production and raise the food close to where it will be consumed.

c. Use local food production that is sustainable, and reduce the chemicals and genetically altered crops used.

d. Try to find a balance of using some chemicals, genetic engineering, and organic farming that is not as harmful to the environment.

e. Do something else. Explain

Name: _____   Date: _____

Chapter One: Food Production Issues

Food Production Issue Discussion Sheets

- -

Issue 3 – Usable Land and Water

Twenty-eight percent of Earth's surface is land; the other 72% is water.

Of the 28% that is land, only 19% is biologically productive, while 9% is only marginally productive or unproductive. Land is biologically productive if it is fertile enough to support agriculture, forests, or animal life. The marginally productive or unproductive land includes pavement, land covered by ice, land that has no water, or land that has unsuitable soil conditions for plant growth. The total area of biologically productive land is about 10 billion hectares. This is the amount of land that is available to provide food, water, and other resources for all living things.

Of the 72% of Earth's surface lakes and oceans, only 4% is biologically productive for human use. The other 68% is marginally productive or unproductive. The productivity of water is reduced by destruction of coral reefs, oil spills, overfishing, and shoreline development.

Recent changes in global weather patterns have brought new challenges to food production. Desertification is one challenge. **Desertification** is the erosion of formerly productive land into deserts. The most famous example of desertification in the United States was the Dust Bowl in the 1930s. Due to poor farming techniques and a long drought, much of the land in Kansas, Oklahoma, and Texas literally blew away. Today, desertification is causing the Sahara desert to expand south across Africa at a rate of 48 km per year. This land goes from being biologically productive to unproductive.

Question: There is a shortage of food in the world. What should be done?

a. Use chemicals to make the marginally productive areas more productive.

b. Clear more forestland for farming.

c. Halt development in or near lakes, rivers, and oceans and decrease pollution to preserve the productivity of the water areas.

d. Design new technologies that would increase food production without harming the environment.

e. Do something else. Explain

Name: _____   Date: _____

Chapter One: Food Production Issues

Food Production Issue Discussion Sheets

- -

Issue 4 – Hydroponics

Hydroponics is growing plants in nutrient solutions without soils. Nutrients are dissolved in water and directly absorbed into the roots. Nutrients can be formulated so that plants always take in the nutrients needed. An inert material, such as coconut husks, gravel, or mineral wool, may be used to provide support for the plant and add air so the nutrient solution can circulate to the plant's roots.

The advantages of hydroponics include that is it a more efficient use of water and fertilizers, it uses a minimal amount of land area, and environmental pollution is minimized. Disease and pests can be prevented as soil is not required. Also, the water in the system can be reused, thus, lowering the cost of water used for the growth of plants.

The disadvantages of hydroponics are the high cost of starting and operating the hydroponic system, high use of energy, and difficulty setting up effective management of the system. Crops produced must have a high economic value to make them a cost-effective hydroponic crop. The presence of chemical fertilizers and high humidity allows salmonella and other pathogens to grow. Each different type of plant may require different types of fertilizers and growing systems.

Question: There is a shortage of food in the world. What should be done?

a. Design and engineer more hydroponic systems to increase food production.

b. Decrease the use of hydroponics because they can increase salmonella outbreaks and spread other diseases.

c. Design new systems that use natural nutrients for the plants and control the growth of diseases.

d. Do something else. Explain

Name: _____   Date: _____

Chapter One: Food Production Issues

Food Production Issue Discussion Sheets

- -

Issue 5 – Food Processing and Preservation

Food preservation and processing are an important part of food production. Food processing and preservation means the processes by which raw food is made suitable for eating, cooking, storing, marketing, and long shelf life.

In areas where crops cannot be grown year around, there has to be some way to store food to use during the winter months when food cannot be grown. Historically, fish and meats were dried or salted to preserve them. Louis Pasteur developed the pasteurization process for wine and milk, which killed the organisms that caused food to spoil. In the 19th and 20th centuries, food preservation was done by heating and sealing food into jars or cans and by freezing foods.

Not all food is grown locally. Some of the food is transported from other parts of the world. Ways of preserving food for extended periods of time and carrying it through different temperatures had to be developed. One way to preserve food longer and make it easier to transport is by processing the food. Food processing is what occurs to food between the time it is harvested and when it can be consumed. Food processing can be done by heating, freezing, pasteurizing, and adding chemical preservatives.

While the processing and preservation of foods allows it to last longer, these processes require more natural resources, such as water, fossil fuels, and land. Packaging and processing food increases wastes and creates more problems with waste management. Packaging materials break down slowly, and the chemicals from these packages and preservation processes can become highly concentrated in our water, air, and soil.

Question: There is a shortage of food in the world. What should be done?

a. Continue the way food is currently packaged, processed, preserved, and transported.

b. Find ways to reduce the amount of fossil fuels and natural resources used to package, preserve, process, and transport foods.

c. Only eat what can be grown locally, and process and preserve food the way it is done on small, self-sufficient farms—canning, freezing, drying, and smoking food.

d. Do something else. Explain.

Name: _____ Date: _____

Chapter One: Food Production Issues

Food Production Issue Discussion Sheets

- -

Issue 6 – Sustainability of Food Production

     An ideal sustainable food system uses few fossil fuels and uses recycled metals and minerals; protects or enhances biodiversity; enriches soil and protects water quality; avoids using man-made chemicals that stay in the environment longer than a few days; does not use a lot of plastic packaging or invents ways to recycle all packaging; feeds all people without feeding one community at the expense of others; uses resources efficiently; and recycles or reuses wastes.

     If the natural systems that provide humans with oxygen, soil, the absorption of carbon dioxide, clean water, and biodiversity are destroyed, the earth will not support life.

Question: There is a shortage of food in the world. What should be done?

  a. Clear more land and plant as much food as possible, using whatever means are available to produce the food.

  b. Find ways to reduce the use of fossil fuels in crop production, packaging, and transportation while increasing crop production.

  c. Eliminate all food packaging to reduce the use of fossil fuels.

  d. Do something else. Explain

Chapter One: Food Production Issues

Investigate Further: Food Production Issues

TEACHER NOTE: Some references are controversial, so tell students to fact-check sources and claims made in these books or websites. These are placed here to help students understand different attitudes involved in food production and food systems.

Books:

Bowden, Rob. *Food and Water.* Cambridge, MA: Smart Apple Media. 2009.

Casper, Julie Kerr. *Agriculture: The Food We Grow and Animals We Raise.* New York: Chelsea House Publications. 2007.

Charles, Daniel. *Lords of the Harvest: Biotech, Big Money, and the Future of Food.* Cambridge, MA: Perseus Publishing. 2002.

D'Aluisio, Faith and Peter Menzel. *What the World Eats.* Berkeley, CA: Tricycle Press. 2008.

Genetic Modification of Food. New York: Heinemann Library. 2005.

Holt-Gimenéz, Eric. *Food Rebellions: Crisis and the Hunger for Justice.* Oakland, CA: Food First Books. 2009.

Kerr, Jim. *Food: Ethical Debates on What We Eat.* Cambridge, MA: Smart Apple Media. 2008.

Kimbrell, Andrew. *Fatal Harvest: The Tragedy of Industrial Agriculture.* Washington, D.C.: Island Press. 2002.

Mason, Paul. *Food.* New York: Heinemann-Raintree. 2005.

Menzel, Peter. *What I Eat: Around the World in 80 Diets.* Napa, CA: Material World. 2010.

Pollan, Michael. *The Omnivore's Dilemma for Kids: The Secrets Behind What You Eat.* New York: Dial. 2009.

Rooney, Anne. *Feeding the World.* Cambridge, MA: Smart Apple Media. 2009.

Smith, Jeffrey M. *Seeds of Deception: Exposing Industry and Government Lies About the Safety of the Genetically Engineered Foods You're Eating.* Fairfield, IA: Yes! Books. 2003.

Wilson, Michael R. *Hunger: Food Insecurity in America.* New York: Rosen Publishing Group. 2009.

Wolny, Philip. *Food Supply Collapse.* New York: Rosen Publishing Group. 2010.

Websites:

4-H
http://www.4-h.org/

Agriculture in the Classroom: Kids' Zone
http://www.agclassroom.org/kids/index.htm

Bureau of Labor Statistics: Occupational Outlook Handbook, 2010-11 Edition: Agricultural and Food Scientists
http://www.bls.gov/oco/ocos046.htm

Are We Eating Our Way Into a Crisis?
http://myecoproject.org/get-involved/organic-living/

Center for Food Safety
http://truefoodnow.org/

Cool Foods Campaign
http://coolfoodscampaign.org/

Cornell University: Discovering the Food Systems
http://www.hort.cornell.edu/department/faculty/eames/foodsys/index.html

Food First
http://www.foodfirst.org/

Food Security and Dietary Health
http://www.cohabnet.org/en_issue2.htm

Institute of Science in Society: FAO Promotes Organic Agriculture
http://www.i-sis.org.uk/FAOPromotesOrganicAgriculture.php

Chapter One: Food Production Issues

Investigate Further: Food Production Issues

International Center for Food Industry Excellence
http://www.icfie.com/

Mark Winne: High Food Prices: Just Another Bad Day in the Food Line
http://www.markwinne.com/52/

The New York Times: The Spotless Garden
http://www.nytimes.com/2010/20/18/garden/18aqua.html?_r=1

Ocean Arks International: Ecological Food Production
http://www.oceanarks.org/Ecological_Food_Production.php

Organic Consumers Association: Why Industrialized & Globalized Farm and Food Production is Not Sustainable
http://www.organicconsumers.org/BTC/meacher091905.cfm

Rodale Institute: Kids & Families
www.rodaleinstitute.org/organic_kids

Sustainable Food Center
http://www.sustainablefoodcenter.org/

Sustainweb: 7 Principles of Sustainable Food
http://www.sustainweb.org/sustainablefood/

United Nations: Food and Agricultural Organization
http://www.fao.org/

    22 countries in protracted crisis
    www.fao.org.news/sroy/en/item/46114/icode/

    Dramatic changes in global meat production could increase risk of human diseases
    http://www.un.org/apps/news/story.asp?NewsID=23824&Cr=livestock&Cr1=

U.S. Department of Agriculture
http://www.usda.gov/

Economic Research Service: State Fact Sheets
http://www.ers.usda.gov/statefacts/

Agriculture Research Service: Sci4Kids
http://www.ars.usda.gov/is/kids/

Farm Service Agency: FSA Kids
http://www.fsa.usda.gov/FSA/kidsapp?area=home&subject=landing&topic=landing

U.S. Food and Drug Administration: Science and Our Food Supply
http://www.fda.gov/Food/ResourcesForYou/StudentsTeachers/ScienceandTheFoodSupply/default.htm

U.S. Working Group on the Food Crisis
http://usfoodcrisisgroup.org/

What's On My Food?
http://www.whatsonmyfood.org/

Why Hunger? Local and Regional Food Systems
http://www.whyhunger.org/programs/fslc/topics/local-a-regional-food-systems/faqs.html

Video Resources

Food, Inc.
http://www.foodincmovie.com/

The Future of Food
http://www.thefutureoffood.com/

Name: _____   Date: _____

Chapter One: Food Production Issues

Food Production Issues Assessment

Objectives:

Students will be able to…

- Examine their own beliefs and values to make decisions related to food production.
- Debate the issues, respecting the rights of others to maintain different rights and values.
- Evaluate possible solutions to food production issues.
- Explain what needs to be considered when making decisions about managing food production.

1. Describe four issues related to food production.

_____

_____

_____

_____

2. What is the best way to increase food production for a growing population with the least amount of damage to the environment and human health?

_____

_____

_____

_____

_____

_____

_____

3. When deciding how to increase food production, what needs to be considered?

_____

_____

_____

_____

_____

_____

Chapter Two: Biologically Productive Land & Water

Teacher Information

Topic: Natural Resources—Biologically Productive Land and Water

Standards:
NSES – Unifying Concepts and Processes
Systems, Order, and Organization
Form and Function

NSES – Content
NSES A: Science as Inquiry
NSES B: Physical Science
NSES C: Life Science
NSES D: Earth and Space
NSES E: Science and Technology
NSES F: Personal and Social Perspectives
NSES G: Science as a Human Endeavor

NCTM:
Problem Solving
Communication
Reasoning
Mathematical Connections
Probability

ITEA:
Nature of Technology
Technology and Society
Technological World

Concepts:
Amount of land and water on Earth
Biologically productive land and water
Biologically unproductive land and water
Marginally productive land and water
All living things must have land and water to survive.

Objectives:
Students will be able to…
- Explain why it is important to conserve our natural resources.
- Explain how much of Earth's surface is land and water.
- Describe how much land is biologically productive.

Activity 1–Productive Land and Water (p. 19–20)
Materials:
Chart paper   Markers   Rulers
Pencils   Colored pencils

Activity 2–Biologically Productive Water (p. 21–27)
Materials:
World Map   5-gallon container   Water
Classroom set of *One Well: The Story of Water on Earth* by Rochelle Strauss (Tonawanda, NY: Kids Can Press Ltd. 2007.)

Per Group:
Calculators   16-oz. container
Plastic cup (smaller than 16-oz.)
Tablespoon   Eyedropper

Activity 3–Ecological Footprint (p. 28–30)
Materials:
Ecological footprint calculator. These can be found online or in other sources. (See activity for list of sources.)

Chapter Two: Biologically Productive Land & Water

Student Information

Topic: Natural Resources—Biologically Productive Land and Water

Concepts:
Amount of land and water on Earth
Biologically productive land and water
Biologically unproductive land and water
Marginally productive land and water
All living things must have land and water to survive.

Objectives:
Students will be able to…
- Explain why it is important to conserve our natural resources.
- Explain how much of Earth's surface is land and water.
- Describe how much land is biologically productive.

Content Background:

The amount of biologically productive land and water on Earth is very small. Earth has a surface area of 51 billion hectares (2.47 acres in one hectare). This amount of land needs to provide food, water, and other resources for everyone on Earth. Twenty-eight percent of the surface of the Earth is land; the other 72% is water. Of the 28% that is land, only 19% is biologically productive, while 9% is only marginally productive or unproductive.

Land is **biologically productive** if it is fertile enough to support agriculture, forests, or animal life. The marginally productive or unproductive land includes pavement, land covered by ice, land that has no water, or land that has unsuitable soil conditions for plant growth. The total area of biologically productive land is about 10 billion hectares.

Of the 72% of Earth's surface lakes and oceans, only 4% is biologically productive for human use. The other 68% is marginally productive or unproductive. The productivity of water may be reduced by destruction of coral reefs, oil spills, overfishing, and shoreline development.

Of the 51 billion hectares of surface area, including land and water, only about 23% or 12 billion hectares is productive land and water. This is the only area available to produce our food, materials, and energy resources and to absorb our wastes. The population of the world is 6.3 billion people. If the biologically productive land and water resources were divided evenly among all the people, the average Earth share would be 1.9 hectares or 4.7 acres.

Every person consumes products and services made from natural resources. Therefore, every person on Earth has an ecological footprint. An **ecological footprint** is defined as the area of

Chapter Two: Biologically Productive Land & Water

Student Information

biologically productive land and water required to produce the resources a person consumes and to absorb the wastes generated by that person.

Ecological footprint calculators vary in the way the footprint is calculated, but all of the calculators examine food supplies, housing, transportation, and consumption or waste management. The average American uses 24 acres (9.6 hectares) to provide for consumption of goods and services. Remember, that if the resources are divided equally for every person on Earth, each person's share would be only 1.9 hectares or 4.7 acres.

There are many things that can be done to reduce one's ecological footprint. Some food-related things include buying locally grown foods, buying organic foods, planting a garden, using reusable bags when shopping, and using fewer processed foods. Buying food grown locally and gardening reduces transportation costs.

Processed foods require a lot of energy and natural resources for packaging and transportation. The processing is done so that the foods last longer and can be transported farther to ar-

eas that cannot grow certain foods. For example, strawberries do not grow in New York in the winter. However, strawberries can be grown in Chile at this time. But it takes a lot of fossil fuels to get the strawberries from Chile to New York. It cuts down on costs and resources used to buy foods grown locally and processed minimally.

Food production depends on human practices, geology, and hydrological and biological cycles and systems. A **food system** is the system by which food is produced, processed, and distributed.

Modern industrial agricultural practices are more productive economically but are not sustainable. Some think these practices threaten the biological systems necessary for life. These practices have caused topsoil erosion, loss of fertility, arable land losses, and losses to insect pests that become immune to the pesticides that have been developed. A **sustainable food system** does not extract minerals from the earth's crust faster than the earth can absorb them.

Name: _____   Date: _____

Chapter Two: Biologically Productive Land & Water

Student Activity

Activity 1 – Productive Land and Water

Challenge Question: How much biologically productive land and water are available for food production, goods, and services?

Materials:

Chart paper   Markers   Rulers   Pencils   Colored pencils

Procedure:

1. Draw a large circle on the chart paper.
2. Divide the circle so that 28% represents the land on Earth and 72% represents the water on Earth.
3. Color 19% of the 28% green to represent the biologically productive land.
4. Color the other 9% brown to represent the nonproductive or marginally productive land.
5. Draw 3–4 small lines from the brown section into the green section to represent productive land that has been lost because of soil erosion, building/urbanization, and desertification.
6. Color 4% of the water blue. This represents the earth's surface lakes and oceans that are biologically productive.
7. Color the other 68% black to represent marginally productive or unproductive areas of water.
8. Draw 3–4 small black lines from the black area into the blue area to represent pollution, destruction of coral reefs, oil spills, and shoreline development that are destroying the biologically productive areas.

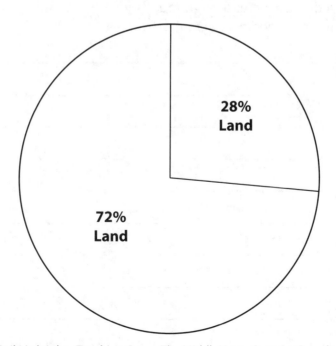

Adapted from Grant, Tim and Gail Littlejohn. *Teaching Green: The Middle Years.* Ontario, Canada: New Society Publishers. 2004.

Name: _____ Date: _____

Chapter Two: Biologically Productive Land & Water

Student Activity

Conclusion:

1. Examine the chart. What percentage of land is available for food production?

   _____

2. Identify some of the problems with food production, waste management, and a growing population.

   _____

   _____

   _____

   _____

   _____

   _____

   _____

   _____

3. How can food production be increased without reducing the amount of biologically productive land and water with harmful food production processes?

   _____

   _____

   _____

   _____

   _____

   _____

   _____

   _____

   _____

Name: _____   Date: _____

Chapter Two: Biologically Productive Land & Water

Student Activity

Activity 2 – Biologically Productive Water: Part 1

Challenge Question: How much of Earth's water is biologically productive?

Materials:
World Map
Classroom set of *One Well: The Story of Water on Earth* by Rochelle Strauss (Tonawanda, NY: Kids Can Press Ltd. 2007.)

Procedure:
Read the book *One Well: The Story of Water On Earth* by Rochelle Strauss.

Discussion:

1. Does all of the water on Earth come from one well? Explain.

    _____

    _____

    _____

    _____

    _____

2. Where is the water on Earth?

    _____

    _____

    _____

    _____

3. How is the earth's water recycled?

    _____

    _____

    _____

    _____

Name: _____   Date: _____

Chapter Two: Biologically Productive Land & Water

Student Activity

4. Create a diagram of the water cycle.

5. How do plants and animals use water?

    _____

    _____

    _____

    _____

    _____

6. How do people use water?

    _____

    _____

    _____

    _____

    _____

Name: _____   Date: _____

Chapter Two: Biologically Productive Land & Water

Student Activity

7. According to the book, where is the highest daily average of water used per person? Why do you think they use the most?

   _____

   _____

   _____

8. According to the book, where is the lowest daily average of water used per person? Why do you think they use the least?

   _____

   _____

   _____

Examine the world map.

9. Explain how the topographical features on the map might help explain why North America uses the most water and Ethiopia uses the least?

   _____

   _____

   _____

   _____

10. How much of the earth's surface is water?

   _____

11. How is the water distributed?

   _____

   _____

   _____

   _____

Name: _____   Date: _____

Chapter Two: Biologically Productive Land & Water

Student Activity

Activity 2 – Biologically Productive Water: Part 2

Materials:
Calculators

Procedure:
Look at the data table below.

Water on Earth	
Source	**Percentage of Total Water**
Oceans	96.54%
Groundwater	
Groundwater – saline/brackish	0.93%
Groundwater – fresh	0.76%
Surface Water	
Glaciers/ice caps	1.74%
Freshwater lakes	0.007%
Saltwater lakes	0.006%
Rivers	0.0002%
Other	
Ground ice, permafrost	0.022%
Atmospheric water vapor	0.001%
Marshes, wetlands (mix of fresh and salt)	0.001%
Soil moisture	0.001%
Incorporated in organisms	0.0001%
Total	~100%

Water on Earth table from: *Project WILD Aquatic.* Houston, TX: Council for Environmental Education. 2003.

Discussion:

1. What source accounts for the largest percentage of the earth's water?

    _____

2. Is the ocean water usable to humans (for example, as drinking water or to irrigate crops)? Explain.

    _____

    _____

    _____

Name: _____   Date: _____

Chapter Two: Biologically Productive Land & Water

Student Activity

Using the table on the previous page, calculate the percent of water available for use by humans.

Freshwater Amounts for Human Use	
Source	**% of Total Water**
Glaciers/ice caps	
Fresh groundwater	
Freshwater lakes	
Rivers	
Total	

3. Are there other life forms that need to use this freshwater too? Explain.

_____

_____

_____

_____

_____

4. How can all species survive with this amount of water?

_____

_____

_____

_____

_____

_____

Name: _____   Date: _____

Chapter Two: Biologically Productive Land & Water

Student Activity

Activity 2 – Biologically Productive Water: Part 3

Materials:

5-gallon container   5 gallons of water
    Per Group:
    Calculators   16-oz. container   Plastic cup (smaller than 16-oz.)
    Tablespoon   Eyedropper

Measurements to Note:

    5 gallons or 1,280 tablespoons will represent all of the water on the Earth.
    5 gallons = 1,280 tablespoons (Tbsp.)
    1/10 Tbsp. = 25 drops
    0.002 of a Tbsp. = less than a drop

Procedure:

1. Calculate the volume of the other quantities provided on the Water on Earth Table on page 24 into tablespoons. Record the quantities in the table below.

    Note: When multiplying percentages, move the decimal to the left before you multiply. For example, the amount of ocean water is 96.54%, so the number you multiply by is 0.9654

    To calculate the number of tablespoons of ocean water, multiply 0.9654 x 1,280 Tbsp. = 1,235.71 Tbsp.

Water on Earth	
Source	**Tablespoons in 5 Gallons**
Oceans	1,235.71 Tbsp.
Groundwater	
Groundwater – saline/brackish	
Groundwater – fresh	
Surface Water	
Glaciers/ice caps	
Freshwater lakes	
Saltwater lakes	
Rivers	
Other	
Ground ice, permafrost	
Atmospheric water vapor	
Marshes, wetlands (mix of fresh and salt)	
Soil moisture	
Incorporated in organisms	
Total	

Water on Earth table and activity from: *Project WILD Aquatic.* Houston, TX: Council for Environmental Education. 2003.

Name: _____ Date: _____

Chapter Two: Biologically Productive Land & Water

Student Activity

2. Calculate the volume of water other than ocean water and saltwater sources in tablespoons.

_____

After you have made your calculations, finish the activity.

3. Put 32 Tbsp. of water into your 16-oz. cup. This represents the freshwater portion of all water. Most of this is locked in glaciers and icecaps or in deep groundwater aquifers.

4. From the 32 Tbsp. of water, remove the accessible freshwater sources—fresh groundwater, rivers, lakes—and place that in the smaller container.

5. From that small container, remove the amount of water representing all freshwater lakes and rivers. Place that into the tablespoon.

6. Extract from the tablespoon the amount representing rivers.

7. How much is left to represent the water found in freshwater lakes?

_____

Conclusion:

1. Why is it important to conserve water?

_____

_____

_____

_____

2. How can we conserve our water resources?

_____

_____

_____

_____

_____

_____

Name:_____   Date:_____

Chapter Two: Biologically Productive Land & Water

Student Activity

Activity 3 – Ecological Footprint

Challenge Question: How big is your ecological footprint?

Materials:
Ecological footprint calculator from one of the following sources.

Grant, Tim and Gail Littlejohn. *Teaching Green: The Middle Years.* Ontario, Canada: New Society Publishers. 2004. (How Big Is Your Footprint? pgs. 84–88)

Adventures With Bobbie Bigfoot
http://www.kidsfootprint.org/

Earth Day Network Footprint Calculator
http://earthday.net/footprint/flash.html

Ecological Footprint Calculator
http://www.myfootprint.org/

Green Schools
http://www.greenschools.net/form.pp?modin=53

School Carbon Footprint Calculator
http://www.dott07.com/flash/dott_024.htm

Zerofootprint KidsCalculator
http://www.zerofootprintkids.com/kids_home.aspx

Procedure:
1. Use one of the ecological footprint calculators to determine your ecological footprint.
2. Create a class graph of the footprints.

If it was distributed evenly, the average Earth share would be 1.9 hectares or 4.7 acres.

3. How do the footprints in your graph compare to the average Earth share?

_____

_____

_____

Chapter Two: Biologically Productive Land & Water

Student Activity

4. Compare your class graph with the table below.

Number of Hectares Consumed by Country	
Country	**Number of Hectares per Person**
United States	10 hectares
Canada	9 hectares
Italy	4 hectares
Pakistan	Less than 1 hectare

5. How does your data compare to the table above?

_____

_____

_____

6. Determine the number of Earths needed if everyone in the world had your footprint. Divide the total number of hectares from your calculation by 1.9 hectares or 4.7 acres. How many additional Earths would be needed?

_____

7. The calculation that you did does not include the other 10 million species that also need the resources in the biologically productive areas of the earth. What do you think would happen to the amount of available resources if these were also added into the total?

_____

_____

_____

_____

Chapter Two: Biologically Productive Land & Water

Student Activity

8.   Currently, 20% of the earth's wealthier nations use 80% of the available resources. What are the implications of this?

_____

_____

_____

_____

_____

_____

Challenges:

1.   Design a solution to the need for more food production while balancing the available land and water resources.

_____

_____

_____

_____

_____

2.   Design a sustainable farm.

_____

_____

_____

_____

_____

_____

Chapter Two: Biologically Productive Land & Water

Investigate Further: Biological Productivity and Ecological Footprint

Books:

Canizares, Susan and Pamela Chanko. *Water*. New York, NY: Scholastic Inc. 1998

Cole, Jenna. *The Magic School Bus: At the Waterworks*. New York, NY: Scholastic. 1986.

Hooper, Meredith. *The Drop in My Drink: The Story of Water on Our Planet*. London: Frances Lincoln Children's Books. 1998.

Jakab, Cheryl. *Ecological Footprints*. New York: Benchmark Books. 2010.

Karas, G. Brian. *On Earth*. New York: Puffin. 2005.

Kent, Kay, Barbara Aston, Myrna Mitchell, Barbara Ann Novelli, and Michelle Pauls. *Sensational Springtime*. Fresno, CA: AIMS Education Foundation. 2007.

Lawrence Hall of Science. *FOSS Science Stories: Water*. Nashua, NH: Delta Education. 2003.

Lindob, David L. *Soil! Get the Inside Scoop*. Madison, WI: American Society of Agronomy. 2008.

Montgomery, David R. *Dirt: The Erosion of Civilization*. Berkeley, CA: University of California Press. 2008.

Project WILD. Houston, TX: Council for Environmental Education. 2007.

Project WILD Aquatic. Houston, TX: Council for Environmental Education. 2005

Rapp, Valerie. *Protecting Earth's Land*. New York: Learner Publications. 2008.

Websites:

Agriculture in the Classroom: Kids' Zone
http://www.agclassroom.org/kids/index.htm

American Community Gardening Association
http://www.communitygarden.org

Brooklyn Botanic Gardens: Composting Basics
http://www.bbg.org/gardening/article/composting_basics/

Care 2 Make a Difference?
http://www.care2.com/channels/ecoinfo/kids

Center for Ecoliteracy
http://www.ecoliteracy.org

City Farmer
http://www.cityfarmer.info

Food First: Institute for Food and Development Policy
http://www.foodfirst.org/

Global Footprint Network
http://www.footprintnetwork.org/

Heifer Project
http://www.heifer.org

ICLEI Global: Local Governments for Sustainability
http://www.iclei.org/

Kids Can Make a Difference
http://www.kidscanmakeadifference.org

Cornell University: Agricultural Outreach and Education
http://agout.cals.cornell.edu/

Kids Gardening
http://www.kidsgardening.com

Natural Resources Defense Council: The Green Squad
http://www.nrdc.org/greensquad/intro/intro_1.asp

The Natural Step
http://www.naturalstep.org/

Ocean Arks International
http://www.oceanarks.org/

U.S. Department of Agriculture: Economic Research Service: Land Use, Value, and Management
http://www.ers.usda.gov/Briefing/LandUse/measuringurbanchapter.htm

Name: _____   Date: _____

Chapter Two: Biologically Productive Land & Water

Biological Productivity Assessment

Objectives:

Student will be able to…
- Explain why it is important to conserve our natural resources.
- Explain how much of the earth's surface is land and water.
- Describe how much land is biologically productive.

Matching:

_____ 1. Biologically productive

_____ 2. Marginally productive or
             unproductive

_____ 3. Ecological footprint

_____ 4. Hectare

_____ 5. Food system

a. 2.47 acres

b. System by which food is produced, processed,
    and distributed

c. Land or water that is fertile enough to support
    agriculture, forests, or animal life

d. Pavement, land covered by ice, land that has no
    water, or land that has unsuitable soil conditions
    for plant growth

f. Calculation of the area required to produce
    resources consumed and assimilate the wastes
    generated by a population and current
    technology

6. Why is it important to conserve natural resources?

_____

_____

_____

_____

_____

7. How much of the earth's surface is water?

_____

_____

Name: _____   Date: _____

8. How much of the water on Earth is usable by humans, plants, and animals?

_____

_____

9. How much of the earth's surface is land?

_____

_____

10. How much of the earth's surface is considered biologically productive?

_____

_____

11. The small amount of biologically productive land and water combined with the growing population creates a problem for the amount of food that can be produced. How can this problem be solved?

_____

_____

_____

_____

_____

_____

_____

_____

_____

_____

_____

_____

_____

Chapter Three: Food Systems, Chains, & Webs

Teacher Information

Topic: Food Systems

Standards:
NSES – Unifying Concepts and Processes
Systems, Order, and Organization
Form and Function

NSES – Content
NSES A: Science as Inquiry
NSES B: Physical Science
NSES C: Life Science
NSES D: Earth and Space
NSES E: Science and Technology
NSES F: Personal and Social Perspectives
NSES G: Science as a Human Endeavor

NCTM:
Problem Solving   Communication
Reasoning   Probability
Mathematical Connections

ITEA:
Nature of Technology
Technology and Society
Technological World

Concepts:
Food system   Food web
Food chain   Systems
Interdependence

Objectives:
Students will be able to…
- Describe a food system and give an example of a food system.
- Explain how energy flows through a food chain.
- Explain how energy flows through a food web.
- Describe foods from the source to consumers.
- Explain that all animals either directly or indirectly need plants for food.
- Create a model of a food chain.

Activity 1 – Food System (p. 36–38)
Materials:
Lunch menu or labels from processed products and fresh produce
Poster paper   Markers   Rulers
Note: Food products are bread, ready-to-eat cereal, juice, applesauce, tomato soup, jam, etc., that have been processed. Fresh produce would be apples, oranges, vegetables, etc., that have not been processed.

Activity 2 – Food Chain (p. 39–41)
Materials:
Owl pellets   Toothpicks   Tweezers
Paper towels   Hand lenses   Balance
Tape measure   Plastic gloves   Ruler
Meat trays or white paper for sorting
Small animal skeleton diagrams
Classroom set of *The Barn Owl* by Sally Tagholm (Boston, MA: Kingfisher. 2003) or another barn owl book; see reference page for other suggestions

TEACHER NOTE: Owl pellets can be picked up in the wild, but the dry pellets must be baked in an oven at 325 degrees for 40 minutes or in a microwave on high for 20 seconds to destroy any parasites that may be in the pellets. Owl pellets can be ordered from a variety of sources. These pellets have been sanitized.

Some sources for owl pellets are:

Genesis, Inc.
Elementary and advanced owl pellet kits have diagrams as well as the pellets.
http://www.pellet.com/view_product.aspx?categoryID=1&subcategoryID=3

Carolina Biological

Ward Scientific

Chapter Three: Food Systems, Chains, & Webs

Student Information

Topic: Food Systems

Concepts:
Food system
Food web
Food chain
Systems
Interdependence

Objectives:
Students will be able to…
- Describe a food system and give an example of a food system.
- Explain how energy flows through a food chain.
- Explain how energy flows through a food web.
- Describe foods from the source to consumers.
- Explain that all animals either directly or indirectly need plants for food.
- Create a model of a food chain.

Content Background:

A **food system** is the system by which food is produced, processed, and distributed. The food is grown, shipped, processed, shipped again to markets, purchased in stores, transported home by consumers, and eaten.

The energy needed for the food system is not just the energy related to transportation, processing, preserving, planting, and harvesting. All of the energy in our food directly or indirectly comes from the sun.

Plants use the energy from the sun to make glucose through a process called photosynthesis. During **photosynthesis**, the chlorophyll in green plants uses the sun's energy to combine carbon dioxide and water to make glucose and oxygen. Animals eat the plants and use the stored energy. Other organisms eat the animals to get nutrition and energy. This is called a food chain.

A **food chain** is the transfer of food energy from one organism to another as each organism consumes a lower member of the chain. The chain is made up of producers and consumers. A **producer** is a green plant that can make its own food.

Consumers are any living things that eat other living things. Consumers include **herbivores**, which only eat plants; **carnivores**, which only eat meat; and **omnivores**, which eat plants and animals. **Decomposers** are consumers that break down plant and animal tissues of dead organisms to return the nutrients to the soil. Examples of decomposers are bacteria and fungi.

An example of a simple food chain is the sun grows a sunflower, a rat eats the seeds, and an owl eats the rat. The sunflower is the producer that takes the energy from the sun and the nutrients from the soil made available by decomposers to make the plant grow. The rat is a consumer. It eats the sunflower seed to get energy for life. The owl eats the rat to get energy for survival. When these animals die, decomposers break down the tissues to again provide the nutrients in the soil to grow more plants. The energy flows from the sun to the sunflower, from the sunflower to the rat, and from the rat to the owl.

Food webs are complex patterns showing the energy flow in an ecosystem based on who eats whom within the system. When food chains overlap and link to each other, a food web is formed.

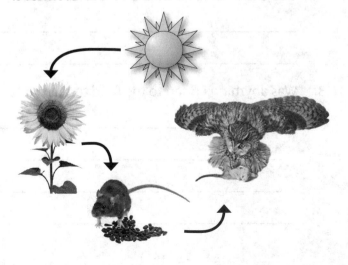

Name: _____ Date: _____

Chapter Three: Food Systems, Chains, & Webs

Student Activity

Activity 1 – Food System

Challenge Question: Where does the food on the table come from?

Materials:
Lunch menu or labels from processed products and fresh produce
Poster paper   Markers   Rulers

Note: Food products are bread, ready-to-eat cereal, juice, applesauce, tomato soup, jam, etc., that have been processed. Fresh produce would be apples, oranges, vegetables, etc., that have not been processed.

Procedure:
1. List the food that you had for lunch.

    _____

    _____

    _____

2. Describe what is in each of the foods.

    _____

    _____

    _____

    _____

    _____

    _____

3. Was anything added to the food to make it look the way that it does? Explain.

    _____

    _____

    _____

    _____

Chapter Three: Food Systems, Chains, & Webs

Student Activity

4. Describe the food system involved with everything on the lunch menu from the growth of the food to the food being consumed. Be sure to include all of the steps involved in a food system: growing, harvesting, storing, transporting, changing (transforming or processing), packaging, marketing, retailing, preparing, and consuming. Use your own paper if you need more room for your answer.

_____

_____

_____

_____

_____

_____

_____

_____

_____

_____

_____

_____

5. On your own paper, make a diagram of that process.

6. What impact did bringing those foods to the table have on the environment?

_____

_____

_____

_____

_____

Name:_____   Date:_____

Chapter Three: Food Systems, Chains, & Webs

Student Activity

7. What natural resources were used to bring that food to the table?

    _____

    _____

    _____

    _____

    _____

    _____

    _____

8. Is there a better way to get the food to the table with less impact on the environment and our natural resources?

    _____

    _____

    _____

    _____

    _____

    _____

    _____

9. Examine all of the diagrams that were drawn. What do you notice about the source of all of the food in the menu?

    _____

    _____

    _____

    _____

    _____

Name: _____   Date: _____

Chapter Three: Food Systems, Chains, & Webs

Student Activity

Activity 2 – Food Chain

Challenge Question: What organisms are in the food chain of an owl?

Materials:

Owl pellets Toothpicks Tweezers Paper towels
Hand lenses Balance Tape measure Ruler Plastic gloves
Meat trays or white paper for sorting Small animal skeleton diagrams
Classroom set of *The Barn Owl* by Sally Tagholm (Boston, MA: Kingfisher. 2003.) or another barn owl book; see reference page for other suggestions

Procedure:

1. Remove the foil from the object.
2. Examine the object with the hand lens. Do not take it apart.
3. Record your observations in the table below.

Mass (g)	Length (cm)	Circumference (cm)	Observations

4. What do you think it is?

   _____

   _____

5. These objects are found on farms around barns. Read *The Barn Owl* by Sally Tagholm or another book on barn owls.

6. After reading the story, what do you think the object is? Explain.

   _____

   _____

   _____

7. What is an owl pellet?

   _____

   _____

Name: _____   Date: _____

Chapter Three: Food Systems, Chains, & Webs

Student Activity

8. On your tray/white paper, use the tools provided to dissect the owl pellet. Look through the materials very carefully. Some of the items in the pellet may be very small and fragile. Record your observations.

    _____

    _____

    _____

    _____

    _____

9. Use the bone charts provided to identify the bones in the pellet. How many different animals did the owl eat? How do you know?

    _____

    _____

    _____

10. Use a hand lens to examine the teeth in the animal skeletons. Describe how the teeth are arranged.

    _____

    _____

    _____

    _____

11. Are the animals you found carnivores, herbivores, or omnivores? How do you know?

    _____

    _____

    _____

    _____

    _____

Name: _____   Date: _____

Chapter Three: Food Systems, Chains, & Webs

Student Activity

12.   Draw a diagram of a simple food chain for the owl based on what was found in the pellet. Be sure to include the sun in the chain. Label each organism as a producer or consumer and a carnivore, herbivore, or omnivore.

13.   On your own paper, draw a diagram of a possible food web for the owl. Be sure to include the sun in the web.

14.   What happens when one part of the food chain disappears?

   _____

   _____

   _____

   _____

15.   Describe the impact of foods and food processing on wildlife and the environment.

   _____

   _____

   _____

   _____

   _____

16.   Why is it important for agricultural engineers to understand food chains and webs?

   _____

   _____

   _____

   _____

   _____

Challenge:
On your own paper, design a food web diagram showing the energy flow of food to a human.

Chapter Three: | Food Systems, Chains, & Webs

Further Investigation: Food Systems, Chains, and Webs

Books:

Ansberry, Karen and Emily Morgan. *Picture Perfect Science Lessons.* Alexandria, VA: National Science Teacher's Association. 2010.

Gray, Susan Heinrichs. *Food Webs: Interconnecting Food Chains.* New York: Compass Points Books. 2008

Heinz, Brian. *Butternut Hollow Pond.* Minneapolis, MN: Millbrook Press. 2005.

Hooks, Gwendolyn. *Makers and Takers: Studying Food Webs in the Ocean.* Florida: Rourke Pub. 2008.

Kalman, Bobbie. *Food Chains and You.* New York: Crabtree Publishing. 2004

Lauber, Patricia. *Who Eats What? Food Chains and Webs.* New York, NY: Harper Collins. 1994.

McGinty, Alice B. *Carnivores in the Food Chain.* New York: PowerKid Press. 2002

Project WILD. Houston, TX: Council for Environmental Education. 2007.

Project WILD Aquatic. Houston, TX: Council for Environmental Education. 2005

Riley, Peter. *Food Chains.* Danbury, CT: First Avenue Editions. 2010.

Slade, Suzanne. *What Do You Know About Food Chains and Food Webs?* New York: PowerKid Press. 2008

Solway, Andrew. *Food Chains and Webs.* Florida: Rourke Pub. 2009.

Websites:

Agriculture and Food Systems
http://www.sustainable.org/economy/agriculture-a-food-systems

BBC: GCSE Bitesize: Food Chains
http://www.bbc.co.uk/schools/gcsebitesize/science/add_aqa/foodchains/foodchains1.shtml

BBC: Sea Life: Blue Planet Challenge
http://www.bbc.co.uk/nature/blueplanet/webs/flash/main_game.shtml

Chain Reaction: Build a Food Chain
http://www.ecokids.ca./pub/eco_info/topics/frogs/chain_reation/index.cfm

Chipper Woods Bird Sanctuary: Owls and Owl Pellets
http://www.wbu.com/chipperwoods/photos/owls.htm

Cornell University: A Primer on Community Food Systems
http://www.hort.cornell.edu/department/faculty/eames/foodsys/primer.html

Enchanted Learning: Food Chains and Food Webs
http://www.enchantedlearning.com/subjects/foodchain/

The Food Trust
http://www.thefoodtrust.org

Geography4Kids.com: Another Link in the Food Chain
http://www.geography4kids.com/files/land_foodchain.htm

Gould League: Build Your Own Food Webs
http://www.gould.edu.au/foodwebs/kids_web.htm

Identify the Food Chains
http://www.cas.psu.edu/DOCS/WEBCOURSE/WETLAND/WED1/identify.html

Kidwings
http://www.kidwings.com/owlpellets/flash/v4/index.htm

The Owl Pages: Digestion in Owls
http://www.owlpages.com/articles.php?section=owl+physiology&title=Digestion

PBS: The Living Edens: Feed Me
http://www.pbs.org/edens/etosha/feedme.htm

Sustainable Food Systems
http://www.sustainablefoodsystems.com

World Owl Trust
http://www.owls.org/Information/pellets.htm

Name: _____ Date: _____

Chapter Three: Food Systems, Chains, & Webs

Food Systems, Chains, & Webs Assessment

Objectives:

Students will be able to…

- Describe a food system and give an example of a food system.
- Explain how energy flows through a food chain.
- Explain how energy flows through a food web.
- Describe foods from the source to consumers.
- Explain that all animals either directly or indirectly need plants for food.
- Create a model of a food chain.

Matching:

_____ 1. Food chain

_____ 2. Food web

_____ 3. Omnivore

_____ 4. Carnivore

_____ 5. Herbivore

_____ 6. Producer

_____ 7. Consumer

_____ 8. Food system

_____ 9. Decomposers

a. System by which food is produced, processed, and distributed

b. Eats meat only

c. Transfer of food energy from one organism to another as each organism consumes a lower organism

d. Eats only plants

e. Eats plants and animals

f. Makes its own food, i.e., green plants

g. Cannot make its own food, depends on the producers or other animals for food

h. Consumers that break down dead plant and animal tissues to make nutrients for the soil

i. Overlapping food chains that are linked together

10. Give an example of a food system.

_____

_____

_____

Name: _____   Date: _____

11.   Draw and label a diagram of a food chain. Explain how the energy flows through the food chain.

12.   Select one thing that you had for lunch today and explain how the food got from the source of the
      food to your plate.

      _____

      _____

      _____

      _____

      _____

      _____

      _____

13.   Explain why all food comes either directly or indirectly from plants.

      _____

      _____

      _____

      _____

14.   Explain why all energy in food comes from the sun.

      _____

      _____

      _____

      _____

Chapter Four: Food and Energy

Teacher Information

Topic: Food and Energy

Standards:
NSES – Unifying Concepts and Processes
Systems, Order, and Organization
Form and Function

NSES – Content
NSES A: Science as Inquiry
NSES B: Physical Science
NSES C: Life Science
NSES D: Earth and Space
NSES E: Science and Technology
NSES F: Personal and Social Perspectives
NSES G: Science as a Human Endeavor

NCTM:
Problem Solving
Communication
Reasoning
Mathematical Connections

ITEA:
Nature of Technology
Technology and Society
Technological World

Concepts:
Food and energy
Food chain
Food web
Calories and energy
Making decisions about eating right

Objectives:
Students will be able to…
  • Explain how food and energy are related.
  • Describe how energy flows through a food chain.
  • Explain how consuming a nonvegetarian diet would affect the amount of energy available.
  • Design a healthy diet plan.

Activity – Accounting for Energy Consumed (p. 48–51)
TEACHER NOTE: Upper-Middle/High School—There is an open flame, so this activity requires supervision. It should be done away from all flammable materials in a well-ventilated area.

CAUTION!—HEALTH HAZARD: This procedure involves nuts. If any students are allergic to nuts, they should not remain in the classroom and should be excused from this lab. Inform students in other classrooms or adjoining science laboratories or students who may use the same lab for other classes.

Materials: (Per group)
Triple-beam or double-pan balance and masses
Thermometer
Graduated cylinder/measuring cups
One large test tube
Matches
Tongs
Large metal spoon with insulated handle
50 mL of water
50-mL Pyrex test tube
2 almonds
Baby carrot
Safety goggles
Gloves
Ring stand and buret clamp or test tube holder to hold the test tube
Alcohol burner/candle

Chapter Four: Food and Energy

Student Information

Topic: Food and Energy

Concepts:
Food and energy
Food chain
Food web
Calories and energy
Making decisions about eating right

Objectives:
Students will be able to…
- Explain how food and energy are related.
- Describe how energy flows through a food chain.
- Explain how consuming a nonvegetarian diet would affect the amount of energy available.
- Design a healthy diet plan.

Content Background:

All living organisms need energy to live. Energy is needed for all voluntary as well as involuntary functions. This energy is obtained from food that is consumed. Food also provides us with nutrients, minerals, vitamins, and proteins.

Due to an increasing world population, there is a need for more food production. World food production more than doubled from 1950 to 1984. However, the average food production per capita has decreased by more than 20%. The reasons for this decrease are due to population growth, more nonvegetarian diets, and natural factors like droughts and a decrease in soil fertility.

Energy from food is released by the metabolism of food in living organisms. The energy flow through living organisms starts with sunlight and photosynthesis, and then travels through the food chain in small amounts. Producers, primary consumers, secondary consumers, tertiary consumers, and decomposers are all part of the food chain. As the energy moves through a food chain, the amount of energy transferred diminishes.

Figure 1 demonstrates how energy flows from the sun to consumers. At each level in a food chain, 10% of the energy is passed to the next organism. Most of the energy (90%) is lost in the form of heat. The amount of energy transferred to the next level of the food chain is one tenth of the amount it receives from the previous level.

Chapter Four: Food and Energy

Student Information

Producers receive the maximum amount of energy from the sun (10%). One percent is transferred from the producer level to the **primary consumer** (the first animal to eat it). The **secondary consumer** receives 0.1%, and the **tertiary** (third) **consumer** receives 0.01%, and so on. The higher the level on the food chain, the less energy there is available. Living organisms located at the top of the food chain require a large amount of food to meet their energy needs. Figure 1 shows the flow of energy through a food chain.

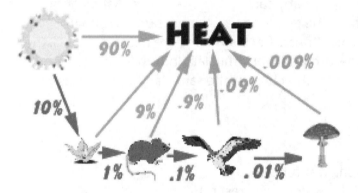

Figure 1: Energy Flow in a Food Chain

Energy from food is produced through the process of cellular respiration. Energy produced is measured in calories. A **calorie** (abbreviated cal.) is the amount of energy or heat required to raise the temperature of 1 gram of water by 1 degree Celsius or 1.8 degrees Fahrenheit. The number of calories present in food demonstrates the amount of potential energy in food. When the food is **metabolized** (broken down), the potential energy (calories) is released in a form of energy that can be used for all functions for living things.

For example, if 100 calories is stored in 100 grams of soybeans, and one living organism consumes the 100 grams of soybeans, the living organism is able to retain only 10 calories from the soybeans. The rest of the 90 calories are lost as heat and waste. If the same 100 grams of soybeans are fed to hogs, the hogs gain 10 calories. Then if another living organism consumes the hog, the living organism gains only 1 calorie. The next living organism to consume whatever has consumed the hog will receive less than 1 calorie when the energy is transferred to the next level.

You can see that consumption of a non-vegetarian diet yields very few calories for energy in a living organism. Because very few calories are transferred in the higher consumer levels, it is essential that individuals eat more vegetables, since vegetables contain more energy.

Name: _____   Date: _____

Chapter Four: Food and Energy

Student Activity

Activity – Accounting for Energy Consumed

Challenge Question: How can energy in foods be calculated?

Materials:
NOTE: There is an open flame in this activity, so adult supervision is required. The activity should be done away from all flammable materials in a well-ventilated area.

Each group needs to have the following items:
Triple-beam or double-pan balance and masses   Graduated cylinder/measuring cups
Thermometer   One large test tube   Matches   Tongs
Large metal spoon with insulated handle   50 mL of water   Gloves
50-mL Pyrex test tube   2 almonds   Baby carrot   Safety goggles
Ring stand and buret clamp or test tube holder to hold the test tube   Alcohol burner/candle
CAUTION!—HEALTH HAZARD: This procedure involves nuts. If any students are allergic to nuts, they should not remain in the classroom and should be excused from this lab. Inform students in other classrooms or adjoining science laboratories or students who may use the same lab for other classes.

Procedure:
Step 1
a. Wear safety goggles.
b. Measure 25 mL of water and pour into the 50-mL test tube.
c. Measure and record the initial temperature of the water in the test tube.
d. Measure and record the mass of two almonds
e. Look at the almond bag and record the number of calories two almonds have in the observation section below.

Figure 2: Setting of Test Tube on a Clamp Stand

Step 2
a. Hold the two almonds under the test tube in the spoon and light them with a match, the candle, or the alcohol burner.
b. Make sure the test tube containing the water is over the burning almonds.

Name: _____　　Date: _____

Chapter Four: Food and Energy

Student Activity

Figure 3a and 3b: Setup of Experiment

3a: The Materials to Use (test tube/boiling tube,
clamp stand, spoon, test tube holder)

3b: Burning Almonds Under the Tube

Step 3
a.　Burn the almonds for two minutes under the test tube.
b.　Measure and record the temperature of water in the test tube.

Step 4
Conduct steps 1 to 3 again with one baby carrot. Dry the carrot with a paper towel first.

Observations: Record your observations in the table provided.

1.　Number of calories for two almonds as listed on the package. _____

Type of Food	Mass of Food (g)	Mass of Water in (g) 1 mL = 1 g	Initial Temperature of Water (C)	Final Temperature of Water (C)

2.　Use the formula below to calculate the amount of energy released per gram in joules and then in calories. **Note:** The star sign (*) stands for the mathematical multiplication operation.

A **joule** is the unit in which energy is measured. It actually measures the amount of electrical energy in the food. 1 calorie = 4.184 joules. 1 kilocalorie (kcal) = 4.184 kilojoules (kJ).

Energy released from food/gram:

$$\frac{\text{joule (J)} = \text{mass of water in grams (g)} * \text{temperature rise in degrees (° C)} * 4.2}{\text{Mass of food in grams (g)}}$$

Name: _____ Date: _____

Chapter Four: Food and Energy

Student Activity

The answer above can be changed to *calories,* the common word used for the energy released, by multiplying the answer by 0.239 as listed below (converting from joules to calories).

Energy released from food in food per gram joule (J) * 0.239 calories =
Amount of calories released

The value 4.2 is the specific heat capacity of water, in joules per gram per degree Celsius—the number of joules taken to raise the temperature of water by 1 degree C. 1 cm^3 of water has a mass of 1 g and is also equal to 1 mL.

1 joule is the same as 0.239 calories. 1 calorie = 4.184 joules.

Amount of calories released = the number of joules (J) * 0.239 calories

Note: The unit for measuring energy is joules, but we talk about calories when food is discussed. A calorie is the amount of energy needed to raise the temperature of 1 cm^3 (or 1 g) of water by 1° C. Most individuals know that, on average, a healthy diet needs between 1,000 and 2,000 *calories* per day. However, in food package labels, calories are stated as *kilocalories* (kcal) or *Calories,* which means 1 kilocalorie = 1,000 calories.

Conclusion:

1. What does a living organism do with the energy released from the food consumed?

   _____

   _____

   _____

   _____

2. What was the original source of energy in the foods that were tested?

   _____

3. Why might the amount of energy be different in the almonds and in the carrot?

   _____

   _____

   _____

   _____

Name: _____   Date: _____

Chapter Four: Food and Energy

Student Activity

4. Were the calorie values listed on the almond package different from what you found out? If, so explain why.

_____

_____

_____

_____

5. What can be done to the experimental setup to obtain more accurate results for the amount of energy released from food?

_____

_____

_____

_____

6. What information does an individual need to know about food, calories, and energy to avoid wasting energy?

_____

_____

_____

_____

7. School age children need 1,600–2,500 calories per day. What will happen if children consume excess calories?

_____

_____

_____

_____

Challenges:
1. On your own paper, design a diet that would provide a person with the needed amount of calories.
2. On your own paper, design a healthy lifestyle plan.

Chapter Four: Food and Energy

Further Investigation: Food and Energy

Books:

Burstein, John. *Energy In, Energy Out: Food as Fuel.* New York: Crabtree Publishing. 2008.

VanCleave, Janice. *Food and Nutrition for Every Kid.* New York: Wiley. 1999.

Websites:

The Accidental Scientist: Science of Cooking
http://www.exploratorium.edu/cooking/index.html

BBC and Nutrition
http://www.bbc.co.uk/health/treatments/healthy_living/nutrition/index.shtml

Cornell University: Discovering the Food System
http://www.hort.cornell.edu/department/faculty/eames/foodsys/

Dietary Recommendations for Healthy Children
http://www.heart.org/HEARTORG/Getting Healthy/Dietary-Recommendations-for-Healthy-Children_UCM_303886-Article.jsp

Discovery Health: How Calories Work
http://health.howstuffworks.com/wellness/diet-fitness/weight-loss/calorie.htm

Food and Energy and Strategies for Sustainable Development
http://www.unu.edu/unupress/unupbooks/80757e/80757e00.htm

Important Food Basics: Energy
http://www.healthyeatingclub.org/info/books-phds/books/foodfacts/html/data/data2a.html

KidsHealth: Learning About Calories
http://kidshealth.org/kid/stay_healthy/food/calorie.html

KidsHealth: What's a Vegetarian?
http://kidshealth.org/kid/stay_healthy/food/vegetarian.html

Merck: Food Additives and Contaminants
http://www.merck.com/mmhe/sec12/ch152/ch152e.html

National Heart Lung and Blood Institute: Balance Food and Activity
http://www.nhlbi.nih.gov/health/public/heart/obesity/wecan/healthy-weight-basics/balance.htm

Science & Health Education Partnership: Measuring Calories in Food
http://www.seplessons.org/node/349

The Science of Energy Balance: Calorie Intake and Physical Activity
http://science.education.nih.gov/supplements/nih4/energy/default.htm

TLC Cooking: How Food Works
http://recipes.howstuffworks.com/food.htm

TLC Cooking: What are calories?
http://recipes.howstuffworks.com/question670.htm

U.S. Food and Drug Administration
http://www.fda.gov/NewsEvents/Testimony/ucm096475.htm

What Does 200 Calories Look Like?
www.wisegeek.com/what-does-200-calories-look-like

World Food Programme: Food Quality Control
http://foodquality.wfp.org/FoodNutritional Quality/Energy/tabid/114/Default.aspx?Page Contentmode=1

Name: _____   Date: _____

Chapter Four: Food and Energy

Food and Energy Assessment

Objectives:
Students will be able to…
- Explain how food and energy are related.
- Describe how energy flows through a food chain.
- Explain how consuming a nonvegetarian diet would affect the amount of energy available.
- Design a healthy diet plan.

Matching:

_____ 1. Energy

_____ 2. Organism

_____ 3. Food

_____ 4. Food chain

_____ 5. Consumer

_____ 6. Producer

_____ 7. calorie

_____ 8. joule

_____ 9. One kilocalorie
           or Calorie

a. Transfer of food energy from one organism to another as each organism consumes a lower organism

b. Cannot make its own food, depends on the producers or other animals for food

c. Any living thing

d. Has the ability to make its own food, i.e., green plants

e. A unit of heat; the amount of heat needed to raise the temperature of one gram of water one degree Celsius.

f. Equal to 1,000 calories, used to describe the amount of energy available from food

g. Unit of work and all other forms of energy

h. Provides living things with energy, nutrients, minerals, vitamins, and proteins

i. Ability to do work

10. Describe how food and energy are related.

_____

_____

_____

_____

Name: _____ Date: _____

11. Describe how energy flows through a food chain.

_____

_____

_____

_____

_____

12. Explain how consuming a nonvegetarian diet would affect the amount of energy available to the consumer.

_____

_____

_____

_____

13. Design a healthy diet plan for a day that would take in 1,600–2,500 calories.

_____

_____

_____

_____

_____

14. Describe what would happen if you exceeded the recommended amount of calories taken in every day.

_____

_____

_____

15. Is diet enough to maintain a healthy lifestyle? Explain.

_____

_____

_____

_____

Chapter Five: Farming

Teacher Information

Topic: Farming

Standards:

NSES – Unifying Concepts and Processes
Systems, Order, and Organization
Form and Function

NSES – Content
NSES A: Science as Inquiry
NSES B: Physical Science
NSES C: Life Science
NSES D: Earth and Space
NSES E: Science and Technology
NSES F: Personal and Social Perspectives
NSES G: Science as a Human Endeavor

NCTM:
Problem Solving
Communication
Reasoning
Mathematical Connections
Probability

ITEA:
Nature of Technology
Technology and Society
Technological World

Concepts:
Usable land
How many acres does it take to grow enough food for the population?
Crop selection
Types of farming
Farming—organic vs. chemical, crop rotation, soil, plants, livestock, genetic engineering, environmental impact
Composting
Pesticides, herbicides

Objectives:
Students will be able to…
- Describe farming throughout history.
- Explain the impact of using chemical fertilizers on the soil, water, environment, and crops.
- Explain the difference between organic and chemical farming.
- Explain the advantages and disadvantages of using chemical pesticides, herbicides, and fertilizers.

Activity 1 – Chemical Farming (p. 59–61)
Materials: (Per Group)
Clear plastic container (size of a shoe box)
5 c. Topsoil   1 c. Sand
1–2 Tbs. Cornstarch   2 plastic vials
Iodine   Eyedropper
Spray bottle
(Note: a drink bottle can also be used)
2–4 c. Water

Activity 2 – Organic Farming (p. 62–64)
Materials: (Per Group)
2 Clear plastic containers (size of a shoebox)
2 c. Sand
2 c. Compost materials (leaves, grass, small pieces of fruit and vegetable scraps)
10 c. Topsoil (Do not use potting soil because it has been sterilized.)
1 c. Water
Graduated or measuring cups
600 mL Measuring beaker or measuring cup
Seeds (lettuce, Wisconsin fast plants, lima beans, or radishes grow fairly quickly)
Ruler
A place outside in the sun where these containers may sit undisturbed

Chapter Five: Farming

Student Information

Topic: Farming

Concepts:
Usable land
How many acres does it take to grow enough food for the population?
Crop selection
Types of farming
Farming—organic vs. chemical, crop rotation, soil, plants, livestock, genetic engineering, environmental impact
Composting
Pesticides, herbicides

Objectives:
Students will be able to…
- Describe farming throughout history.
- Explain the impact of using chemical fertilizers on the soil, water, environment, and crops.
- Explain the difference between organic and chemical farming.
- Explain the advantages and disadvantages of using chemical pesticides, herbicides, and fertilizers.

Content Background:

For thousands of years, people gathered and hunted their food. This worked in areas with small populations and a good source of plants and animals for food. As the population grew, the food became scarce and habitats for wildlife disappeared. People had to develop a way to provide more food and better nutrition.

Ten or eleven thousand years B.C.E, agriculture was established in the Fertile Crescent of the Middle East. **Agriculture**, or farming, is cultivating the soil, growing crops, and raising livestock. Wheat, barley, lentils, and chickpeas were cultivated. This region also had wild goats, sheep, pigs, and cattle that were domesticated for food. The cattle were

also used as work animals, and the manure was used for fertilizer. **Fertilizer** is a substance used to make soil more fertile.

As people began to plant these crops, they also needed to develop ways to harvest and store crops. The first pots were developed in 7,000 B.C.E, in what is now Turkey. This allowed people to save crops for eating and seeds for planting. The plow was developed in 3,500 B.C.E, in Sumeria. This helped people plant more crops, making more food available for more people.

Farmers could not produce everything that they needed, so they used their crops to barter with neighbors who produced the things they did not. **Bartering** was used before currency was developed. It is an exchange of goods or services for other goods or services.

As societies and transportation developed, food became a **commodity** (economic good) to be traded. Ships carried spices from the Middle East, wine and olive oil from Greece, and grain from Egypt. Rome depended on wheat from Egypt and North Africa. In 350 B.C.E., public bakeries were established, beginning one of the first mass production and distribution systems for food.

In the Middle Ages, food production grew with developments in technology. One of these developments was a heavy plow that could till the soil more efficiently, allowing for more grain to be produced. In the eleventh century, gristmills powered by wind and water were developed to grind grain, providing a larger-scale process for turning grain into flour than just grinding by hand.

In Medieval Europe, farmers practiced crop rotation. One year a field would be used for crops.

Chapter Five: Farming

Student Information

The next year it would be used for pasture so that the manure from the animals in the pasture would revitalize the soil. In the later Middle Ages, farmers discovered that **legumes** (plants such as clover, peas, and beans) added nitrogen to the soil. Rotating grain, legumes, and **fallows** (off years) increased productivity of the farms. Adding legumes also added new vegetables to the European diet.

Columbus discovered America while looking for a trade route to India to reduce dependency upon Arabian spices. In America, other crops such as maize (corn), potatoes, tomatoes, and peppers were found and brought back to Europe.

In England, land ownership was privatized and crop and animal production increased. Marshlands were drained for cultivation of crops. The increased land available and production of cheaper food helped feed the **urban** (city) populations of England.

In the eighteenth and nineteenth centuries, science and technology again played a key role in the development of food production. Mineral and chemical fertilizers were developed to help renew the soil. New inventions such as the seed drill, mechanical reapers, tractors, and electric milking machines also increased food production. Advances in science and technology helped scientists develop a better understanding of the nutritional values of food and what was required for a balanced diet. During this time, scientists and engineers found ways to add vitamins and minerals to processed food.

The tractor was invented in the early 1900s  but was not used widely for farming until after World War II. After the war, factories that had produced tanks, airplanes, ammunition, and so on were not needed. These factories started producing tractors and other farm machinery on a wider scale. This industrialization of farming allowed more land to be cultivated in less time. However, as farmers started using tractors, fewer animals were used to plow fields and plant and harvest crops, so there was less **organic** (natural) fertilizer for the fields.

The practice of crop rotation continued. Corn would be planted one year and soybeans would be planted the next year. Soybeans have nitrogen-fixing bacteria on the roots, which adds nitrogen back into the soil after the corn has taken it out.

During World War, II chemists worked with chemicals to kill the enemy. After the war, it was discovered that many of these chemicals could be used for synthetic pesticides, herbicides, and fertilizers. **Pesticides** kill insects and other pests, and **herbicides** kill weeds.

The environmental and human impact of the use of these chemicals is just now being understood. Research shows an increase in cancer rates world-wide. There is a growing body of evidence linking cancer to environmental contamination. In *Living Downstream*, scientist Sandra Steingraber describes her research and investigation of the impact of chemicals on the environment and human health. Steingraber is a biologist who experienced cancer at age 20. She linked the cancer to environmental contamination from chemicals that were upstream from her water supply. She examined toxic release data and cancer registry data and found that there seemed to be a link between the data.

Rachel Carson described the impact of the chemical insecticide DDT on the environment in her book *Silent Spring*. Carson worked for the United States Fish and Wildlife Service. In her book, she described the impact of chemicals such as DDT on bird eggs and other wildlife. Carson's research

Chapter Five: Farming

Student Information

shows a need to examine the environmental and human impact of the chemicals we are creating.

From 1950 to 1980, 80% of the increase in food production was from increasing the amount of land used to increase productivity. Since 1980, all of the increase in grain production has been accomplished from biological technology or genetic engineering to increase crop yields. This was a move from a resource-based agricultural system to a science-based agricultural system.

In the 1990s, advances in biotechnology led to genetically altered crops. **Genetic engineering or bioengineering** of crops may make them resistant to insects and immune to herbicides used to reduce the

amount of weeds in the fields. Genetic engineering can also modify the crop to insert traits that are beneficial to consumers. These might include adding vitamins to fortify the food. Genetic manipulation of crops is controversial because no one knows the long-term effects of eating these genetically altered crops or of eating animals that have eaten altered crops. Governments closely monitor the genetic engineering of crops to prevent misuse of this technology.

Modern industrial farming has become big business in the world market. More efficient agricultural production can lead to low prices and financial losses for food producers. Government subsidies pay farmers to protect them from foreign competition. This keeps farmers in business, but increases food costs. In the United States, sugar costs twice what it does in world markets to allow American farmers to make a living.

Modern industrial agricultural practices are more productive economically but are not sustainable. Some think these practices threaten the biological systems necessary for life. These practices have caused topsoil erosion, loss of fertility, arable land losses, and losses to insect pests that become immune to pesticides. The use of fossil fuels for large farms has polluted the air and created a larger need for imported oil.

Food production is a complex issue. As the population increases, more food is needed. Some ways to increase productivity are to use more land, use chemical engineering to create fertilizers, and use bioengineering to create more productive disease-resistant breeds of plants. Another way to increase food production is to make marginally productive areas more productive by adding nutrients to the soil with chemicals or practices such as crop rotation.

However, scientists have discovered that some of the chemicals used to increase food production are harmful to humans. Some people believe that going back to natural organic farming, using compost and other natural materials as fertilizer, and creating more small local farms to grow food locally is the direction that should be taken. The disadvantage of this practice is there is not as much variety in the diet because different kinds of food need different climates to grow. Not all types of foods can be grown locally in every location.

Scientists and engineers are currently trying to solve the problem of how to produce enough food for the growing population without contaminating the environment and becoming a hazard to humans. This chapter will examine current farming techniques and their impact on the environment.

Name: _____   Date: _____

Chapter Five: Farming

Student Activity

Activity 1 – Chemical Farming

Challenge Question: How do chemical fertilizers, pesticides, and herbicides get into our lakes and streams?

Materials:
Clear plastic container (size of a shoe box)
5 c. Topsoil   1 c. Sand   1–2 Tbs. Cornstarch   2 Plastic vials
Iodine   Eyedropper   2–4 c. Water
Spray bottle (Note: a drink bottle can also be used)

Procedure:
1. Mix 2 c. topsoil and 1 c. sand.
2. Spread the topsoil/sand mixture in the bottom of the plastic container.
3. Spread the remaining 3 c. of topsoil on top of the sand/soil mixture. On one end, create a depression to serve as a lake. Either slope the land toward the lake or raise the land end of the container 1 cm. Fill the lake with water.

4. Let the water settle for at least 5 minutes.
5. Use an eyedropper to remove some water from the lake.
6. Place the water into one of the vials.
7. Put a few drops of iodine in the water in the vial to test for leachate.
8. Label the vial Before Fertilizer (cornstarch).
9. Set the vial with the water and iodine aside.

Name: _____   Date: _____

Chapter Five: Farming

Student Activity

10. Record your observations.

_____

_____

Leachate is the water that collects contaminants as it trickles through wastes, pesticides, herbicides, or fertilizers. Leaching may occur in farming areas, feed lots, or landfills. This may result in hazardous substances entering surface water, groundwater, or soil. As it rains and the water drains over or through the dirt, it may go into lakes, streams, or groundwater. In this experiment, if a leachate is present in the lake, the iodine will turn black.

Is there a leachate present in the lake? How do you know?

_____

_____

11. Sprinkle the cornstarch on top of the soil, but do not put any into the lake. This simulates the addition of chemical fertilizer, pesticide, or herbicide to the field. **NOTE:** To simulate a liquid fertilizer, you may also mix the cornstarch in water and spray it on. Just avoid spraying the lake portion of your simulated farm.

12. Using the spray bottle or a drink bottle, spray the topsoil with water until the cornstarch disappears. Spray it slowly to allow some of the water to be absorbed into the soil.

Name: _____ Date: _____

Chapter Five: Farming

Student Activity

13. Use the eyedropper to remove some of the lake water.
14. Place the water in the second vial.
15. Label the second vial After Fertilizer.
16. Put 4–5 drops of iodine in this water.

17. Record your observations.

_____

_____

18. Compare the first vial with the second vial.

_____

_____

_____

19. Was the leachate present in the second vial? How do you know?

_____

_____

Conclusion:
Explain how chemical fertilizers, pesticides, and herbicides may contaminate oceans, lakes, streams, and groundwater.

_____

_____

_____

_____

_____

Name: _____   Date: _____

Chapter Five: Farming

Student Activity

Activity 2 – Organic Farming

Challenge Question: How does adding compost to soil impact the growth of plants?

Materials:
2 Clear plastic containers (size of a shoebox)
2 c. Sand
2 c. Compost materials (leaves, grass, small pieces of fruit and vegetable scraps)
10 c. Topsoil (Do not use potting soil because it has been sterilized.)
1 c. Water
Graduated cylinder or measuring cups
600 mL Measuring beaker or measuring cup
Seeds (lettuce, Wisconsin fast plants, lima beans, or radishes grow fairly quickly)
Ruler
A place outside in the sun where these containers may sit undisturbed

Procedure:
Soil With Compost
1. Mix 2 c. topsoil and 1 c. sand.
2. Put it in the bottom of the container.
3. Add the compost on top of the sand/soil mixture 2–5 cm deep.
4. Cover the compost with 2–5 cm of topsoil.
5. Plant seeds in the topsoil.
6. Add 1/2 c. of water to the soil.

Name: _____   Date: _____

Chapter Five: Farming

Student Activity

Soil With No Compost

1. Mix 2 c. topsoil and 1 c. sand.
2. Put it in the bottom of the container.
3. Cover the sand/soil mixture with 4–10 cm of topsoil.
4. Plant seeds in the topsoil.
5. Add 1/2 c. of water to the soil.

NOTE: If the containers are placed outside in a rainy season, tops can be made from two 2-liter bottles with the top and bottom cut off. These are open on both ends to allow air into the field. Once the plants grow to the cover, they will have to be removed. The plastic is tied on to be sure the wind does not blow the covers off.

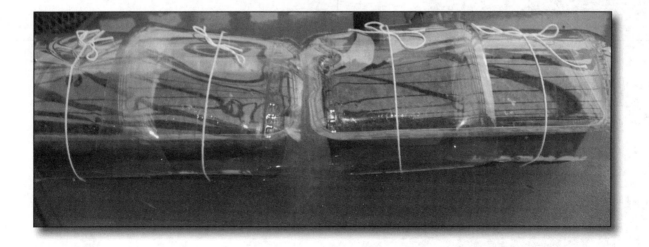

Name:_____ Date:_____

Chapter Five: Farming

Student Activity

Observations:

Construct a data table to record observations. Sample tables are shown below. You will have to make tables with enough spaces for however many days you observe the plants growing.

Soil With Compost Observations		
Date	**Height of the plant (cm)**	**Observations**

Soil With No Compost Observations		
Date	**Height of the Plant (cm)**	**Observations**

Challenge:

Design a growing system that would produce more food without the use of chemical fertilizers.

Chapter Five: Farming

Further Investigation: Farming

Books:

Baines, John. *Food and Farming*. New York: Smart Apple Media. 2008.

Carlson, Laurie. *Green Thumbs: A Kid's Activity Guide to Indoor and Outdoor Gardening*. Chicago: Chicago Review Press. 2010.

Carson, Rachel. *Silent Spring: 40th Anniversary Edition*. New York, NY: Mariner Books. 2002.

Featherstone, Jane. *Earth Alert!: Farming*. New York: Hodder Wayland. 2001.

Goodman, Polly. *Earth in Danger: Farming*. New York: Hodder Wayland. 2005.

Rodger, Ellen. *Reduce Your Footprint: Farming, Cooking, and Eating for a Healthy Planet*. New York: Crabtree Publishing. 2010.

Smith, Angela. *The Effects of Farming*. New York: Franklin Watts, LTD. 2006.

Steingraber, Sandra. *Living Downstream*. Cambridge MA: DaCapo Press. 2010.

Tudge, Colin. *Food for the Future*. New York: Dorling Kindersley Publishing, Inc. 2002.

Wilkes, Angela. *A Farm Through Time: The History of a Farm From Medieval Times to the Present Day*. New York: Dorling Kindersley Publishing, Inc. 2001.

Websites:

4-H: Virtual Farm
http://sites.ext.vt.edu/virtualfarm/main.html/

Agriculture in the Classroom: Kids' Zone
http://www.agclassroom.org/kids/index.htm

Agropolis Museum: Food and Agricultures of the World
http://museum.agropolis.fr/english/default.htm

Growing a Nation: A History of American Agriculture
http://www.agclassroom.org/gan/timeline/index.htm

The Life and Legacy of Rachel Carson
http://www.rachelcarson.org/

Natural Resources Defense Council: The Story of *Silent Spring*
http://www.nrdc.org/health/pesticides/hcarson.asp

Rutgers University: From Farm to Fork
http://njaes.rutgers.edu/health/farmtofork.asp

From Our Farm: Teaching Kids About Food, Nutrition, and the Farm
http://gloucester.njaes.rutgers.edu/fchs/fromourfarms.html

Thinkquest: Apples to Zucchinis: The Story of Food
http://library.thinkquest.org/C001722/farming.html

U.S. Department of Agriculture
http://www.usda.gov/

Agriculture Research Service: Sci4Kids
http://www.ars.usda.gov/is/kids/

Farm Service Agency: FSA Kids
http://www.fsa.usda.gov/FSA/kidsapp?area=home&subject=landing&topic=landing

U.S. Food and Drug Administration: Science and Our Food Supply
http://www.fda.gov/Food/ResourcesForYou/StudentsTeachers/ScienceandTheFoodSupply/default.htm

Name: _____ Date: _____

Chapter Five: Farming

Farming Assessment

Objectives:

Students will be able to…

- Describe farming throughout history.
- Explain the impact of using chemical fertilizers on the soil, water, environment, and crops.
- Explain the difference between organic and chemical farming.
- Explain the advantages and disadvantages of using chemical pesticides, herbicides, and fertilizers.

Matching:

_____ 1. Agriculture

_____ 2. Organic farming

_____ 3. Fertilizer

_____ 4. Crop rotation

_____ 5. Bartering

_____ 6. Legumes

_____ 7. Pesticide

_____ 8. Industrial farming

_____ 9. Herbicide

_____ 10. Fallow

_____ 11. Chemical farming

_____ 12. Urban

_____ 13. Bioengineering

_____ 14. Commodity

a. Having to do with the city

b. Plants such as clover, peas, and beans that add nitrogen to the soil

c. An economic good that people buy, sell, or trade

d. An exchange of goods and services for other goods and services; trading

e. Alternating what is planted in a field each year to prevent the soil from wearing out

f. Use of chemical fertilizers, pesticides, and herbicides to increase food production

g. Letting a field go unplanted for a year

h. Genetically engineering crops to increase food production or to insert beneficial traits

i. A substance used to make soil more fertile

j. A chemical used to kill insects and other pests in crops

k. Using natural materials as fertilizer for crop production

l. A chemical used to kill weeds

m. Large-scale farming that mass-produces crops and livestock

n. Cultivating the soil, growing crops, and raising livestock; farming

Name: _____ Date: _____

15. Explain why farming and food production have changed over time.

_____

_____

_____

_____

16. Explain how science and technology have changed the way food is produced.

_____

_____

_____

_____

17. Explain the advantages and disadvantages of using chemical fertilizers, pesticides, and herbicides.

_____

_____

_____

_____

18. How can more food be produced without having a negative impact on the environment?

_____

_____

_____

_____

_____

Chapter Six: Hydroponics

Teacher Information

Topic: Hydroponics and Food Production

Standards:

NSES – Unifying Concepts and Processes
Systems, Order, and Organization
Form and Function

NSES:
NSES A: Science as Inquiry
NSES B: Physical Science
NSES C: Life Science
NSES D: Earth and Space
NSES E: Science and Technology
NSES F: Personal and Social Perspectives
NSES G: Science as a Human Endeavor

NCTM:
Problem Solving
Communication
Reasoning
Mathematical Connections

ITEA:
Nature of Technology
Technology and Society
Technological World

Concepts:
Hydroponics
Designing a system
Testing solutions
Types of hydroponic systems
What a plant needs to survive

Objectives:
Students will be able to…
• Explain what hydroponics is.
• Describe how plants are cultivated with hydroponics.
• Describe different types of hydroponic systems.

Activity 1 – Water Culture Hydroponics System (p. 72–76)
Materials:
Miracle Grow™ fertilizer or some other fertilizer (Mix with water according to the directions on the package.)
Seeds (lima bean seeds, raw peanuts, corn, Wisconsin fast plants, or other seeds)
Water   1-cm Graph paper
Paper towels
Quart size resealable plastic bag
Stapler   Rulers
Hand lens   1-L Bottle
16-cm long and 5-cm wide strip of polyester quilt batting (cork, Styrofoam, or other inert material) to support the plant
Warm, sunny place

Activity 2 – Hydroponics (p. 77–79)
Materials: (Per group)
3 large-mouth 500-mL Plastic containers without lids, labeled A (distilled water), B (tap water), and C (wet topsoil)
300 mL of Topsoil   300 mL of Distilled water
300 mL of Tap water   15 White basil seeds
Graduated cylinder   Ruler

TEACHER NOTE: You do not need special hydroponic seeds or plants for this experiment; any seed will work. Rice grains may be used for this activity, as long as the rice grains are not treated and are bought from a natural seed or food store.

Chapter Six: Hydroponics

Student Information

Topic: Hydroponics and Food Production

Concepts:
Hydroponics
Designing a system
Testing solutions
Types of hydroponic systems
What a plant needs to survive

Objectives:
Students will be able to…
- Explain what hydroponics is.
- Describe how plants are cultivated with hydroponics.
- Describe different types of hydroponic systems.

Content Background:

Hydroponics is a Greek word that means "water" (*hydro*) and "work" (*ponics*). Hydroponics systems grow plants without soil. Hydroponic systems date back to at least 1627, when Francis Bacon mentioned plants growing without soil. In 1699, John Woodword discovered that plants grew better in nonpurified water as compared to purified water. In 1842, Julius von Sachs and Wilhelm Knop in Germany identified nine essential elements for plant growth in hydroponic systems.

Growing plants using a mineral solution is called **solution culture**. Currently 17 elements have been identified as required elements in a hydroponic solution. What is needed depends upon what is being grown. There are nine **macronutrients** needed: carbon, hydrogen, oxygen, sulfur, phosphorus, calcium, magnesium, potassium, and nitrogen. Relatively large amounts of these macronutrients are needed. Small amounts of eight **micronutrients** are needed. These are iron, zinc, copper, manganese, boron, chlorine, cobalt, and molybdenum.

The first successful use of large-scale hydroponics was on Wake Island in the Pacific Ocean.

Wake Island does not have soil that will grow food. In the 1930s, Pan American Airlines stopped on the island to refuel, and they needed food for the passengers. Hydroponic systems were successfully developed there to grow food. As in this case, new technologies are often developed to fill a need.

Hydroponics refers to plants growing without any kind of soils that contain clay or silt. Hydroponic plants can grow in other mediums. Some of these mediums include water with nutritional substances added, husks of coconuts, gravel, or mineral wool.

In traditional plant growth, soil contains nutrients that plants need to grow and provides support to the roots and plant. When it rains, these nutrients are dissolved in water and carried to the plant through the roots. The type of soil and the amount of nutrients in the soil determine how much of the nutrients the plants can absorb and how well they grow.

In hydroponics, nutrients can be dissolved in water and directly absorbed by the roots. The amount of nutrients can be formulated so that the plant can always take in exactly the nutrients that it needs. An **inert material**, one that has no nutritional value to the plant, is used to provide support for the plant and add air to the nutrient solution to provide oxygen to the plant's roots. Some possible inert materials are polyester quilt batting, Styrofoam, or cork.

Hydroponic systems are classified by how the nutrient-filled water is provided to the plants. These hydroponic systems include water culture, aeroponics, and aggregate.

Water culture systems are the only true hydroponic systems. The plants are grown in a water or water-based system. The plants are supported from above the water so that the roots are suspended in the nutrient solution with the stem above. Some houseplants such as the peace lily can be grown with this system.

Chapter Six: Hydroponics

Student Information

Figure 1: Water Culture Hydroponics System

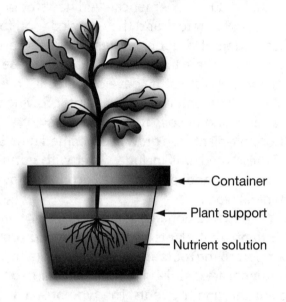

In an **aeroponic system**, the plant's roots are suspended in the air and the nutrient solution is periodically sprayed on the roots. Plants like lettuce, tomatoes, cucumbers, and melons have been grown with this type of system.

In an **aggregate system**, the plant's roots are anchored in an aggregate—inert material like sand, gravel, small stones, vermiculite (super-heated mica), perlite (super-heated volcanic rock), or rock wool. The nutrient solution is circulated through the aggregate material. The plants absorb the nutrients in the solution. Aggregate systems can grow lettuce, tomatoes, green beans, peppers, herbs, carrots, and broccoli. Different types of aggregate systems are classified by how the nutrients are "fed" to the roots. Aggregate systems are gravity flow, sub-irrigation, or wick.

The **gravity flow system** uses gravity to move the nutrient solution through the system. The growing solution is placed above the system containing the plants, and a plastic tube at the bottom of the nutrient container is placed into the plant system. When the valve is opened, the nutrient solution flows through the plant chamber and out a hole in the bottom of the chamber through another tube into another container. This is sometimes called a flood and drain technique. The nutrient solution that is drained off can be reused.

Figure 2: Aeroponic System

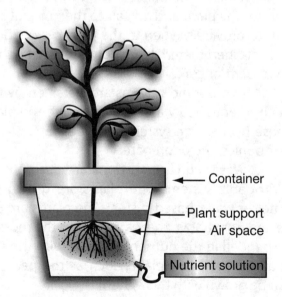

Figure 3: Gravity Flow System (Aggregate)

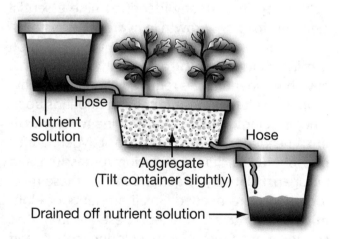

Chapter Six: Hydroponics

Student Information

A **sub-irrigation system** is also a flood and drain technique. This system uses a pump run by a timer to pump nutrients from a nutrient reservoir under the plant chamber to flood the plant container. The chamber is flooded when the pump is on and drains back into the solution reservoir when the pump is off. As the nutrients drain back into the reservoir, air is pulled into the plant's root area, bringing in oxygen to the roots.

Figure 4: Sub-irrigation System (Aggregate)

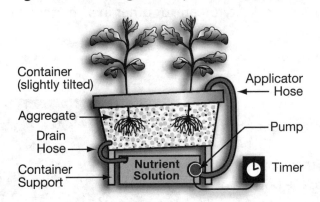

Wick systems have a water-absorbent wick that is put through the bottom of the plant's container into the pot below that contains the nutrient solution. The wick pulls up the solution into the aggregate where it can be absorbed by the roots.

Figure 5: Wick System (Aggregate)

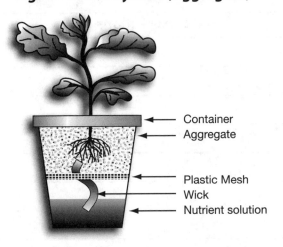

Some large-scale hydroponic systems are enclosed in a greenhouse-like structure, which provides temperature control, cuts down on loss of water due to evaporation, and provides pest and disease control. There are two kinds of operating systems that have been used in large-scale hydroponic systems: opened and closed systems. In an **open system**, the water mineral solution is not reused. In a **closed system**, the water mineral solution is recovered and recycled through the system.

The advantages of hydroponics are that it provides a more efficient use of water and fertilizers, a minimum use of land area, and minimized environmental pollution. Disease and pests can be prevented, as soil is not required. The water in the system can be reused, thus lowering the cost of water used for the growth of plants.

The major disadvantage of hydroponics is the high cost of starting and operating the systems. There is a high use of energy, and setting up effective management systems for successful crop production can be difficult. Different systems are required for different kinds of plants. The crops produced must have a high economic value to make them cost-effective to grow with hydroponics. For example, tomatoes have a high economic value, so it is cost-effective to produce tomatoes using hydroponics.

Other problems include the increased likelihood of *salmonella* growth due to the presence of fertilizer and high humidity. Verticillium wilt can also result from the high humidity, causing pathogens to grow.

Agricultural engineers design ways to increase food production through the use of different growing mediums. The following investigations will explore several different types of hydroponic systems.

Name: _____   Date: _____

Chapter Six: Hydroponics

Student Activity

Activity 1 – Water Culture Hydroponics System

Challenge Question: Can plants grow without soil?

Materials:

Miracle Grow™ fertilizer or some other fertilizer (Mix with water according to the directions on the package.)

Seeds (lima bean seeds, raw peanuts, corn, Wisconsin fast plants, or other seeds)

Water	1-cm Graph paper	Quart size resealable plastic bag
Paper towels	Stapler	Rulers
Hand lens	1-L Bottle	

16-cm long and 5-cm wide strip of polyester quilt batting (cork, Styrofoam, or other inert material) to support the plant

Warm, sunny place

Procedure:

Part 1: Preparing the Plants

1. Place the graph paper on top of the paper towel, and put both into the resealable bag.
2. Staple five times across the width of the bag 5–10 cm from the bottom of the bag so the seeds will not fall through to the bottom of the bag.
3. Put water into the bag. (Just enough to make sure the paper towel is saturated.)
4. Select some seeds to grow.
5. Place the seeds in the bag so the plants are far enough apart to grow.
6. Observe the seeds until roots begin to grow. Then record your observations in the chart below until the plants have a stem 3–4 cm long.

Germination Observations

Date	Length of the Plant (cm)	Observations

Name: _____ Date: _____

Chapter Six: Hydroponics

Student Activity

Germination Observations (cont.)

Date	Length of the Plant (cm)	Observations

Results:

1. How fast did the first seed germinate?

   _____

2. What is the rate of growth of this plant?

   _____

3. Do all of the seeds grow at the same rate? Explain.

   _____

   _____

   _____

4. Do roots and stems grow at the same rate? Explain.

   _____

   _____

   _____

Name: _____ Date: _____

Chapter Six: Hydroponics

Student Activity

Part 2: Plant Growth/Hydroponics

1. When one of the plants from Part 1 has roots and a stem at least 3-4 cm long, carefully remove the plant from the bag. Try to protect the root hairs because they are very important for plant growth.
2. Mix water with Miracle Grow™ or other fertilizer according to the directions on the package.
3. Fill a 1/2-liter or 1-liter bottle full of the water/fertilizer solution.
4. Fold the quilt batting in half lengthwise to make a 2.5-cm by 16-cm strip.
5. Wrap a strip of quilt batting around the stem, being careful not to wrap the roots.
6. Place the plant in the neck of the bottle so it stays up and does not fall into the bottle. Make sure the roots are in the solution.

   This is a simulation of a water culture hydroponics system

7. Make sure that the bottle stays completely full by carefully removing the plant and adding more water as needed. This also allows more oxygen to get to the roots. Be careful when putting the plants back into the bottle that the roots are not damaged.
8. Let the water culture hydroponics system sit in a warm, sunny place.

Name: _____ Date: _____

Chapter Six: Hydroponics

Student Activity

9. Record your observations in the chart below.

Water Culture Hydroponics Observations

Date	Length of the Plant (cm)	Observations

Results:

1. What is the rate of growth for the plant?

    _____

2. How fast did the root grow?

    _____

3. How fast did the leaves grow?

    _____

Name: _____   Date: _____

Chapter Six: Hydroponics

Student Activity

Conclusion:

1. What is hydroponics?

    _____

    _____

    _____

    _____

    _____

2. What do plants need to grow?

    _____

    _____

    _____

    _____

    _____

    _____

3. How would you redesign your water culture hydroponics system to increase crop production?

    _____

    _____

    _____

    _____

    _____

    _____

    _____

    _____

Name: _____   Date: _____

Chapter Six: Hydroponics

Student Activity

Activity 2: Hydroponics

Challenge Question: Which kind of medium (distilled water, tap water, or wet topsoil) promotes the growth of basil?

Materials: (Per group)
3 large-mouth 500-mL Plastic containers without lids
Label the plastic containers A (distilled water), B (tap water), and C (wet topsoil).
300 mL of Topsoil
300 mL of Distilled water
300 mL of Tap water
15 White basil seeds
Graduate cylinder
Ruler

Procedure:
Step 1
Add 5 basil seeds to each of the three containers.

Step 2
Add 300 mL of distilled water to container A.
Add 300 mL of tap water to container B.
Add 300 mL of wet soil to container C.

Step 3
Place containers A, B, and C in an area where the temperature is about 70 degrees Fahrenheit, but make sure it is in the shade because algae can grow in the containers if exposed to sunlight.

Step 4
Observe any growth activity in containers A, B, and C.

Setup of Experiment

Name: _____   Date: _____

Chapter Six: Hydroponics

Student Activity

Observations:

Create an observation table like the sample below, and record your observations every two days for the next month. Your table should have at least 15 lines for each container.

Date	Container A	Height	Observations	Any Inference
Date	**Container B**	**Height**	**Observations**	**Any Inference**
Date	**Container C**	**Height**	**Observations**	**Any Inference**

Results:

1. How many days did the basil seeds take to start growing in containers A, B, and C?

   _____

   _____

   _____

2. What kind of growth did you observe in containers A, B, and C?

   _____

   _____

   _____

3. What are some differences in the growth observed in the seeds in containers A, B, and C?

   _____

   _____

   _____

Name: _____   Date: _____

Chapter Six: Hydroponics

Student Activity

Conclusion:

1. Explain why there are differences in the plants in containers A, B, and C.

    _____

    _____

    _____

    _____

    _____

2. Why do we need to investigate hydroponics for plant growth?

    _____

    _____

    _____

    _____

    _____

    _____

3. How can crop production be increased without hydroponics?

    _____

    _____

    _____

    _____

    _____

    _____

Challenge:
Design a hydroponic system to grow tomatoes or some other vegetable.

Chapter Six: Hydroponics

Further Investigation: Hydroponics

Alabama Cooperative Extension System: Hydroponics for Home Gardeners
http://www.aces.edu/pubs/docs/A/ANR-1151/

Alternative Energy Base: Hydroponics in Commercial Food Production
http://www.alternativeenergybase.com/Article/Hydroponics-in-commercial-food-production/787

Aquaponic Gardening: What is Aquaponics?
http://aquaponicscommunity.com/page/what-is-aquaponics

ATTRA: Aquaponics – Integration of Hydroponics with Aquaculture
http://www.aces.edu/dept/fisheries/education/documents/Horticulturesystemsguide.pdf

Basic Hydroponic Systems
http://www.simplyhydro.com/system.htm

Gardening–Tips–Idea.com: Learning about Hydroponics for Kids
http://www.gardening–tips–idea.com/HydroponicsforKids.html

Grodan: Hydroponics in Education
http://www.grodan101.com/sw63114.php

Hydroponic Experiments for Kids
http://www.grodan101.com/sw63175.php

Growell Hydroponics
http://www.growell.co.uk/pr/60/Deep-Water-Culture-It-s-all-about-the-bubbles-.html

Hydrofarm: Introduction to Hydroponics
http://www.hydrofarm.com/kb_introtohydro.php

Hydro for Hunger
http://www.hydroforhunger.org

Hydroponics Classroom: Hydroponics 101
http://www.hydroponicsclassroom.com/hydroponics_101.html

Hydroponics Simplified: Getting Your Garden Growing
http://www.hydroponics-simplified.com/hydroponics-seeds.html

How Stuff Works?: Hydroponics
http://tlc.howstuffworks.com/home/hydroponics.htm

Institute of Simplified Hydroponics
http://www.carbon.org

International Society for Horticulture Science
http://www.ishs.org

KidsGardening: Exploring Classroom Hydroponics
http://www.kidsgardening.com/HYDROPONICSGUIDE/hydro1-1-intro.asp

Newagehydro
http://www.newagehydro.com/shop/faq.php

Progressive Gardening: Soil-Free Hydroponic Gardening
http://www.progressivegardening.com/soilfreehydroponicgardening.html

Science Tech
http://www.techno-preneur.net/information-desk/sciencetech-magazine/2007/jan07/Hydroponics.pdf

Stealth Hydroponics
http://www.stealthhydroponics.com

Wisconsin Fast Plants
http://www.fastplants.org/

Name: _____ Date: _____

Chapter Six: Hydroponics

Hydroponics Assessment

Objectives:

Students will be able to…

- Explain what hydroponics is.
- Describe how plants are cultivated with hydroponics.
- Describe different types of hydroponic systems.

Matching:

_____ 1. Aggregate

a. Plants are grown only in water or water-based nutrient system

_____ 2. Hydroponics

b. Growing plants without soil

_____ 3. Water culture hydroponic system

c. The plant is in an aggregate, and a wick draws the nutrients to the plant

_____ 4. Aeroponics hydroponic system

d. Flood and drain technique pumps a nutrient solution over the roots of the plant and is drained out of the bottom into the reservoir

_____ 5. Aggregate gravity flow hydroponic system

e. Roots are suspended in the air, and the nutrient solution is sprayed periodically on the roots

_____ 6. Aggregate sub-irrigation hydroponics system

f. Uses gravity to move the nutrient solution through the system

_____ 7. Aggregate wick hydroponics system

g. Inert substance such as sand, gravel, small stones, vermiculite, or perlite

8. Describe how a hydroponic system works.

_____

_____

_____

_____

_____

_____

Name: _____ Date: _____

9. Describe three different types of hydroponic systems.

_____

_____

_____

_____

_____

_____

_____

_____

_____

_____

_____

_____

10. Explain the advantages and disadvantages of using hydroponic systems for growing food.

_____

_____

_____

_____

_____

_____

_____

_____

_____

_____

_____

Chapter Seven: Food Processing & Preservation

Teacher Information

Topic: Food Processing and Preservation

Standards:
NSES – Unifying Concepts and Processes
Systems, Order, and Organization
Form and Function

NSES:
NSES A: Science as Inquiry
NSES B: Physical Science
NSES C: Life Science
NSES D: Earth and Space
NSES E: Science and Technology
NSES F: Personal and Social Perspectives
NSES G: Science as a Human Endeavor

NCTM:
Problem Solving
Communication
Reasoning
Mathematical Connections

ITEA:
Nature of Technology
Technology and Society
Technological World

Concepts:
Food processing
Need for food processing and preservation
Methods of food processing
Food preservation processes

Objectives:
Students will be able to…
• Explain why food is processed.
• Explain why there is a need to preserve food.
• Describe the impact of food processing and preservation on the environment.
• Describe different methods of food processing.
• Describe different methods of food preservation.

Activity: Food Processing and Preservation (p. 88–90)
Materials:
Two heads of cabbage
Two apples
Ten spinach leaves
Six plastic trays or plates
Refrigerator
Access to non-air-conditioned environment
Magnifying glass

Chapter Seven: Food Processing & Preservation

Student Information

Topic: Food Processing and Preservation

Concepts:
Food processing
Need for food processing and preservation
Methods of food processing
Food preservation processes

Objectives:
Students will be able to…
- Explain why food is processed.
- Explain why there is a need to preserve food.
- Describe the impact of food processing and preservation on the environment.
- Describe different methods of food processing.
- Describe different methods of food preservation.

Content Background:

Finding ways to preserve foods for later use has been one of the problems that agricultural engineers have tried to solve since the beginning of food production. In areas where crops cannot be grown year around, there has to be some way to store food to use when food cannot be grown. **Food processing** and **preservation** means the processes by which raw food is made suitable for use in cooking, storing, and marketing. Fruits, grains, vegetables, and animals are grown for human and animal consumption. These products are harvested and eaten or taken to a processing plant. Food processing and preservation alters food to preserve it and make it last a longer period of time.

Food processing and preservation can be traced to prehistoric times when food was processed by fermenting, sun-drying, salting, and cooking it by steaming, baking, grilling, etc. The Greeks, Egyptians, and Romans used these techniques to preserve food.

Most grain will keep if it is kept dry, so it can be stored in silos, bins, or other places. Fish and meats need to be dried, salted, or frozen to preserve them.

In the early 19th century, food preservation involved heating and sealing food into jars or cans. In 1863, Louis Pasteur invented the technique of **pasteurization**, which involved partially sterilizing wine to destroy harmful microorganisms, allowing the wine to last longer without affecting its chemical makeup. The pasteurization process was also later used to prevent milk and beer from spoiling.

Steamships and refrigeration were also developed in the 19th century. This allowed shipping food from different parts of the country and to other countries. Food exports went from 4 million tons in the 1850s to 18 million tons by the 1880s. Chicago, Illinois, became the center of the U.S. meatpacking industry when refrigerated railroad cars were added to trains so meat could be shipped all over the United States.

In the 18th and 19th centuries, science and technology played a key role in the development of food production. Advances in science and technology helped scientists develop a better understanding of the nutritional values of food and what was required for a balanced diet. Scientists and engineers also found ways to process and

Chapter Seven: Food Processing & Preservation

Student Information

preserve food for later use and ways to add vitamins and minerals to processed food.

Many of the advances in food processing in the 19th and 20th centuries were developed in an effort to preserve food for military personnel. Armies and navies needed to be able to feed thousands of soldiers and sailors all over the world, so methods were developed to preserve food that could be stored for long periods of time and transported easily.

The first bottling and canning processes were developed because Napoleon wanted a way to feed his army while on the move. World War II and the space program contributed to the development of modern techniques for food processing. Methods like spray-drying, adding color, adding preservatives, precooked meals, frozen foods, and juice concentrates have emerged from these developments.

Lifestyle changes and a desire for convenience have also led to the invention of safe and effective food processing and preservation techniques. Some of these innovations include microwaveable food, instant foods such as pudding, dehydrated foods such as soups that only need water and heat added, and prepackaged dinners. These products decrease the cooking and preparation times required.

There are many benefits of food processing and preservation techniques. One of the main rea-sons for food processing and preservation is because most food is grown and processed far away from where it is consumed. Therefore, it needs to be safely transported to locations where the consumer can access it. In addition, many harmful toxins can be removed from raw food before it reaches the table. Food processing also helps people who need certain kinds of food like gluten-free food and food with no sugar because of medical conditions. During the processing and preservation, nutrients can be added to food to improve its quality. Processing and preservation reduces spoilage of food because fresh food has a greater chance of having microorganisms.

One disadvantage of food processing and preservation is that naturally occurring vitamins and nutrients may be lost or destroyed. Research reports that vitamin C is destroyed by high temperatures, which is why canned foods have little or no vitamin C. Other substances may be added to preserve flavor during processing. Texture-altering agents in processed food may also add calories to food, making it less healthy. Nitrites and sulfates used for preserving food can cause adverse health effects. One example is MSG. Monosodium glutamate (MSG) is a preservative added to foods that may cause an allergic reaction in some people.

During food processing and preservation, there is a danger the food will become contaminated. To avoid this contamination when food is grown, harvested, and delivered to the table, sanitation systems must be in place. Sanitation in processing facilities is very important to the health of the consumers eating the food. The Food and Drug Administration is an agency in the United States that regulates and monitors food production systems and processing facilities to keep the food safe for human consumption.

In recent years there have been *e. coli* and *salmonella* outbreaks from unsanitary processing of food that have caused many people to become ill. Food is processed in food processing plants, but

Chapter Seven: Food Processing & Preservation

Student Information

it is also processed as restaurants prepare fresh foods to serve to customers. There are also strict rules and regulations from agencies such as public health departments to keep the food in restaurants safe to consume.

Consumers also need to follow safe food-handling guidelines in their own homes as they prepare food. Most packages of meats and produce are marked with safe handling instructions.

Finding the right temperature at which to store and process foods and practicing sanitary food handling can prevent food from spoiling and harmful microorganisms from sickening consumers. Food needs to be stored at a temperature below 40° Fahrenheit or above 130° Fahrenheit. The growth of microorganisms occurs as soon as raw food is permitted to exist in the temperature range of 41–130° Fahrenheit. Food should not be thawed at room temperature. It should be thawed in the refrigerator or in cold water. Temperature controls and thermometers can be used to monitor food storage containers. Refrigerators have temperature controls in them to indicate that the refrigerator is keeping the food at the correct temperature.

The pasteurization process is another way that temperature can be used to preserve food. During this process, food like milk is heated to around 162° Fahrenheit for 15 seconds and then cooled quickly. Any microorganism is destroyed, which prevents the milk from spoiling and increases its shelf life. **Blanching** foods before freezing also uses a process similar to pasteurization. Fruits and vegetables are heated and cooled quickly and then frozen.

Most food-processing companies have certification programs for their employees. They are required to be tested on safe food handling. One of the key aspects of effective food handling is to promote areas where employees can wash their hands with soap and warm water regularly. Employees with illnesses should be restricted from being near food. Good personal hygiene is essential to safe handling of food. Effective practices in food handling are covering hair, wearing closed footwear, removing jewelry, wearing gloves, and not chewing gum or tobacco.

Food-processing and preservation facilities should allow only authorized personnel near where food is being handled. Food processing and preservation facilities should have appropriate exhausts and have easy-to-clean areas that are free from rats, insects, pests, drainage problems, odor problems, debris, and refuse. Chemicals used for cleaning, like detergents and sanitizers, need to be safely stored and used in a manner to prevent contamination of food and food contact surfaces. These chemicals need to be stored in a dry, well-ventilated area that is far from food-handling areas. Sanitary guidelines need to be followed at all stages of food processing and preservation.

Different foods are processed differently depending on what the foods are and how they are going to be used. One way of processing fresh food to eat is to simply wash the food to remove organisms and toxins that may have gotten on these products during growth and transport.

Grain is ground into flour and meal to be used in cereal, bread, crackers, and other food items. Sometimes nutritional supplements and preservatives may be added during the processing of the grain.

Chapter Seven: Food Processing & Preservation

Student Information

Fruits and vegetables are processed by physical, chemical, and biochemical means. The physical means of processing fruits and vegetables include heating, cooling, dehydrating (removing water), sterilizing, filtering, using high-pressure canners, and using vacuum containers. The chemical methods of processing are salting, smoking, adding sugar, and adding ethyl alcohol. Biochemical methods involve fermentation.

The two methods of processing milk and milk products are pasteurization and homogenization. Pasteurization destroys bacteria with high temperature treatment at 162° F. Other milk products can have different temperatures for pasteurization. When raw milk is allowed to stand, the fat rises to the top to form a layer of cream on the top. This process is used to create skim, one-percent, and two-percent milk by removing some of the fat that comes to the top. Whole milk has all of the natural fat left in it. **Homogenization** is a mechanical treatment of the fat in milk to break the fat particles into smaller pieces. This blends the milk and fat so the smaller fat particles are evenly dispersed in the liquid. This reduces the tendency of the fat to rise to the top of the milk when it sits.

Meat processing involves temperature control, refrigerating at 38° F, freezing at 0° F, vacuum packing, canning, and fermenting the meat by adding harmless bacteria to lower the pH, which prevents the growth of harmful pathogens. Another means of processing meats is irradiating the meat. **Irradiation** is a pasteurization method involving the exposure of meat to various doses of radiation to kill microorganisms that cause food spoilage. Curing and smoking are two very old methods of processing meats. When meat is **smoked**, moisture on the surface of meat is decreased, preventing microbial growth. **Curing** meats like ham or sausage, involves the addition of mixtures containing salt, nitrites, and other preservatives.

Typically most oils and fats used for food are plant products. The seeds of plants like soybeans, olives, safflowers, corn, and canola are crushed, pressed, and treated to remove oils and fats for consumption. Other fats and oils are extracted from milk, milk products, and animal fat. The methods involved in the processing of oils and fats are pressing, temperature treatment (more than 175° F), water and alkali refining, deodorization, and bleaching.

Scientists and engineers are working on ways to make environmentally friendly food production, processing, preserving, and packaging. Food processing and preserving facilities are highly regulated by laws to reduce the impact on the environment. Some food processing and preservation techniques deplete or harm our natural resources. The consumption of energy to process food could release harmful gases into the atmosphere. Waste products from processing food may include waste water, fertilizers, and salt and sugar solutions. Packaging the food once it is processed also creates wastes.

The following investigation will examine some of the issues related to processing and preserving food.

Name: _____   Date: _____

Chapter Seven: Food Processing & Preservation

Student Activity

Activity: Food Processing and Preservation

Challenge Question: Why is food preservation needed?

Materials:

Two heads of cabbage	Two apples	Ten spinach leaves
Six plastic trays or plates	Refrigerator	Access to non-air-conditioned environment
Magnifying glass		

Procedure:
This investigation needs to last 10 days.

Step 1
1. Place one cabbage, five spinach leaves, and an apple on separate plastic trays or plates in an area that is not air conditioned. The fruit and vegetables need to have access to the outside air.

Step 2
1. Place one cabbage, five spinach leaves, and an apple on separate plastic trays or plates in the refrigerator. These three items should not be touching each other or any other item in the refrigerator.
2. Place them on the same shelf so they are able to have the same temperature environment.

Observations:
1. Let the items sit for 10 days.
2. Record your observations on Day 5 and Day 10 in the tables below.

Day 5

Item (OUTSIDE)	Firmness 1–5 (5 being most firm)	Smell	Any Other Observations
Cabbage			
Spinach			
Apple			
Item (REFRIGERATOR)	**Firmness 1–5 (5 being most firm)**	**Smell**	**Any Other Observations**
Cabbage			
Spinach			
Apple			

Name: _____   Date: _____

Chapter Seven: Food Processing & Preservation

Student Activity

Day 10

Item (OUTSIDE)	Firmness 1–5 (5 being most firm)	Smell	Any Other Observations
Cabbage			
Spinach			
Apple			
Item (REFRIGERATOR)	**Firmness 1–5 (5 being most firm)**	**Smell**	**Any Other Observations**
Cabbage			
Spinach			
Apple			

Results:

1. Explain what happened to the fruit and vegetables after five days in both environments.

   _____

   _____

   _____

2. Explain what happened to the fruits and vegetables after 10 days in both environments.

   _____

   _____

   _____

3. What was the control group in this experiment?

   _____

4. What were the manipulative and responding variables in this experiment?

   _____

   _____

   _____

Name: _____ Date: _____

Chapter Seven: Food Processing & Preservation

Student Activity

5. Which environments caused the fruits and vegetables to deteriorate in freshness? Explain your answer.

    _____

    _____

6. What other kinds of treatments are possible with these fruits and vegetables to ensure the freshness lasts longer?

    _____

    _____

    _____

    _____

7. How long does it take for a cabbage, spinach leaves, and an apple to spoil in the open environment (without air conditioning or heating)?

    _____

    _____

8. How long does it take for a cabbage, spinach, and an apple to spoil left at a lower temperature in the refrigerator?

    _____

    _____

Challenges:

1. Develop packaging for fresh fruits or vegetables that would not have a negative impact on the environment.
2. Will placing the fruits and vegetables in a plastic bag in an open environment impact how long the fruits and vegetables last? Conduct an investigation to find out.

Chapter Seven: Food Processing & Preservation

Further Investigation: Food Processing and Preservation

Books:

Barnett, Anne and Hazel King. *Food Processing.* New York: Heinemann Library. 2008.

Jango-Cohen, Judith. *The History of Food.* Connecticut: Twenty-First Century Books. 2005.

Murray, Julie. *Cocoa Bean to Chocolate.* Edina, MA: Buddy Books. 2006.

Websites:

Braums Dairy: Just For Kids
http://www.braums.com/JustKids/
AllAboutCows2.asp

Cornell University: Milk Processing
http://www.milkfacts.info/MilkProcessing/
MilkProcessingPage.htm

Food Processing.com
http://www.foodprocessing.com/

> **A Historical Timeline of Food Processing**
> http://www.foodprocessing.com/
> articles/2010/anniversary.html

> **Food Safety: A 3-Part Series**
> http://www.foodprocessing.com/
> articles/2010/foodsafety.html

> **Happy 200th Birthday, Can!**
> http://www.foodprocessing.com/
> articles/2010/octobertoops.html

Encyclopædia Britannica: Fats and Oils Processing
http://www.britannica.com/EBchecked/
topic/202405/fat-processing

Encyclopædia Britannica: Meat Processing
http://www.britannica.com/EBchecked/
topic/371756/meat-processing

Food First
www.foodfirst.org

The Food Guide Pyramid
http://kidshealth.org/kid/stay_healthy/food/
pyramid.html

Food Processing Technology
http://www.foodprocessing-technology.com/

How Cooking Oils Are Made
http://www.madehow.com/Volume-1/Cooking-
Oil.html

INPHO: Cereal Processing
http://www.fao.org/inpho/content/fpt/
CEREALS/prbread.htm

**Iowa State University Extension:
Food Irradiation – What is it?**
http://www.extension.iastate.edu/foodsafety/
irradiation/info/MilkProcessing/

Kids' Guide to Food: Food Processing
http://tiki.oneworld.net/food/food5.html

Louis Pasteur
http://www.accessexcellence.org/RC/AB/BC/
Louis_Pasteur.php

MREInfo.com: MREs (Meals, Ready-to-Eat)
http://www.mreinfo.com/us/mre/mres.html

National Center for Home Food Preservation
http://www.uga.edu/nchfp/

Name: _____ Date: _____

Chapter Seven: Food Processing & Preservation

Food Processing and Preservation Assessment

Objectives:

Students will be able to…

- Explain why food is processed.
- Explain why there is a need to preserve food.
- Describe the impact of food processing and preservation on the environment.
- Describe different methods of food processing.
- Describe different methods of food preservation.

Matching:

_____ 1. Pasteurization

_____ 2. Irradiation

_____ 3. Food processing and preservation

_____ 4. Homogenization

_____ 5. Blanching

_____ 6. Smoking meats

_____ 7. Salmonella

_____ 8. Curing meats

a. Processes by which raw food is made suitable for cooking, storing, and marketing

b. Heating food, then cooling it quickly before freezing

c. Mechanical treatment of the fat in milk to break the fat particles into smaller pieces

d. Exposing food to various doses of radiation to kill microorganisms that cause food spoilage

e. Partially sterilizing wine, milk, etc., to destroy harmful bacteria to allow the food to last longer without changing its chemical makeup

f. Adding mixtures of salt, nitrites, and other preservatives to meats such as ham or sausage

g. Preserving meat by exposing it to smoke, which decreases the moisture on the surface and prevents microbial growth

h. Bacteria that may be present on foods and can cause illness or death in people

9. Explain why food is processed and preserved.

_____

_____

(cont. on the next page)

Name: _____   Date: _____

_____

_____

_____

_____

_____

10.   Describe different methods used for food processing and preservation.

_____

_____

_____

_____

_____

_____

_____

_____

_____

11.   Describe some possible impacts of food processing and preservation on the environment.

_____

_____

_____

_____

_____

_____

_____

_____

Chapter Eight: STEM Design Challenge

Teacher Information

Topic: Design a sustainable food system

Standards:

NSES – Unifying Concepts and Processes
Systems, Order, and Organization
Form and Function

NSES – Content
NSES A: Science as Inquiry
NSES B: Physical Science
NSES C: Life Science
NSES D: Earth and Space
NSES E: Science and Technology
NSES F: Personal and Social Perspectives
NSES G: Science as a Human Endeavor

NCTM:
Problem Solving
Communication
Reasoning
Mathematical Connections
Probability

ITEA:
Nature of Technology
Technology and Society
Technological World

Concepts:
Design a sustainable food system
Sustainability

Objectives:
Students will be able to…
- Identify a problem.
- Brainstorm solutions for the problem.
- Select the best solution to the problem.
- Construct a model of the solution.
- Test the model.
- Evaluate the model.
- Redesign the model.
- Test the redesigned model.
- Retest the redesigned model.
- Communicate the results.

Activity: Designing a Sustainable Food System (p. 96–99)
Materials:
Flip chart paper
Markers
Rulers
Pencils
Variety of construction materials

Chapter Eight: STEM Design Challenge

Student Information

Topic: Design a sustainable food system

Concepts:
Design a sustainable food system
Sustainability

Objectives:
Students will be able to…
- Identify a problem.
- Brainstorm solutions for the problem.
- Select the best solution to the problem.
- Construct a model of the solution.
- Test the model.
- Evaluate the model.
- Redesign the model.
- Test the redesigned model.
- Retest the redesigned model.
- Communicate the results.

Content Background:

  This book has presented multiple issues related to food production. Some of the issues were availability of productive land and water resources; politics; global markets; types of farming—organic, chemical, hydroponic, etc.; industrial farms vs. local farms; environmental impact of food systems; livestock management; growing population; food processing and preservation; and transportation. Human practices, i.e., use of convenience foods and poor recycling habits, also impact the food system.

  Geology and the hydrological and biological cycles and systems are issues that need to be examined in developing any solution to the food production problem. Understanding natural cycles helps better understand how to grow food for a growing population without having a negative impact on the environment.

  Modern industrial agricultural practices are more productive economically but are not sustainable. These practices threaten the biological systems necessary for life. Industrial agricultural practices have caused topsoil erosion, loss of fertility, arable land losses, and losses to insect pests that become immune to the pesticides that have been developed.

  A sustainable food system uses less fossil fuels and uses recycled metals and minerals. Fossil fuels, metals, and minerals break down slowly and can become highly concentrated in our water, air, and soil. A sustainable food system protects or enhances biodiversity, enriches soil, and protects water quality.

  If the natural systems that provide humans with oxygen, soil, the absorption of carbon dioxide, clean water, and biodiversity are destroyed, the earth will not support life. Man-made substances and chemicals are not easily broken down by the natural cycles of the earth. They sometimes accumulate in the environment and damage the air, water, and soil. A sustainable food system avoids using man-made chemicals that stay in the environment longer than a few days.

  A sustainable food system must feed all people and not feed one community at the expense of others. Resources should be distributed more evenly to all people. Currently, people in some areas of the world are starving while people in other areas of the world are becoming obese because of an overabundance of food. A sustainable food system should use resources efficiently and turn waste into resources or food.

  In this activity, students will identify a problem related to our food system, brainstorm ideas about how to solve the identified problem, and design a solution, test the solution, evaluate the results of the test, redesign the plan if necessary, and present the plan to the rest of the class for their evaluation.

Name: _____   Date: _____

Chapter Eight: STEM Design Challenge

Student Activity

Activity: Designing a Sustainable Food System

STEM Challenge Problem: You have purchased a plot of land to use for a vegetable garden, but the soil is not suitable for growing plants. Design an alternative growing system that will grow vegetables but will not harm the environment.

Materials:
Flip chart paper   Markers   Rulers   Pencils
Variety of construction materials

Procedure:
1. Identify the problem stated in the STEM Challenge Problem.

   _____

   _____

2. Brainstorm how you might solve the problem and record your ideas.

   _____

   _____

   _____

   _____

3. Identify one idea to test.

   _____

   _____

4. Design a model of the technology that will solve the problem. Draw a diagram of your model on your own paper.

5. Create a plan that states specifically what materials are needed and the steps explaining how they will be used.

   _____

   _____

   _____

Name: _____   Date: _____

Chapter Eight: STEM Design Challenge

Student Activity

_____

_____

_____

_____

_____

6. Construct a model.

7. Test the model.

8. Record your observations in a data table.

9. Analyze the data you collected

_____

_____

_____

_____

10. Evaluate the model. Did the model work? _____

_____

Name: _____   Date: _____

Chapter Eight: STEM Design Challenge

Student Activity

11. Did the model work like you thought it would? If not, identify the problems and explain.

_____

_____

_____

_____

_____

12. Identify solutions to improve your model.

_____

_____

_____

_____

_____

13. Redesign the model and draw a diagram.

Name: _____ Date: _____

Chapter Eight: STEM Design Challenge

Student Activity

14. Construct and test the redesigned model.

15. Record your observations in a data table.

16. Explain how effectively the design changes helped solve the problem.

   _____

   _____

   _____

   _____

17. Is there something else that could be done to improve the design? Explain.

   _____

   _____

   _____

   _____

18. Communicate the results to the rest of the class.

Challenges:

1. Identify one issue related to food production, i.e., organic farming, hydroponics, etc., that could be used to solve one of the problems related to food production. Design a plan to build, develop, and test that solution.

2. Design a food production system to provide food to feed the increasing number of people in the world despite the lack of land to grow food.

Chapter Eight: STEM Design Challenge

Further Investigation: Food Production and Sustainability

Websites:

4-H
http://www.4-h.org/

Agriculture in the Classroom: Kids' Zone
http://www.agclassroom.org/kids/index.htm

Bureau of Labor Statistics: Occupational Outlook Handbook, 2010-11 Edition: Agricultural and Food Scientists
http://www.bls.gov/oco/ocos046.htm

Are We Eating Our Way Into a Crisis?
http://myecoproject.org/get-involved/organic-living/

Center for Food Safety
http://truefoodnow.org/

Cool Foods Campaign
http://coolfoodscampaign.org/

Cornell University: Discovering the Food Systems
http://www.hort.cornell.edu/department/faculty/eames/foodsys/index.html

Food First
http://www.foodfirst.org/

Food Security and Dietary Health
http://www.cohabnet.org/en_issue2.htm

International Center for Food Industry Excellence
http://www.icfie.com/

The New York Times: The Spotless Garden
http://www.nytimes.com/2010/20/18/garden/18aqua.html?_r=1

Ocean Arks International: Ecological Food Production
http://www.oceanarks.org/Ecological_Food_Production.php

Organic Consumers Association: Why Industrialized & Globalized Farm and Food Production is Not Sustainable
http://www.organicconsumers.org/BTC/meacher091905.cfm

Rodale Institute: Kids & Families
www.rodaleinstitute.org/organic_kids

Sustainable Food Center
http://www.sustainablefoodcenter.org/

Sustainweb: 7 Principles of Sustainable Food
http://www.sustainweb.org/sustainablefood/

United Nations: Food and Agricultural Organization
http://www.fao.org/

U.S. Department of Agriculture
http://www.usda.gov/

> **Economic Research Service: State Fact Sheets**
> http://www.ers.usda.gov/statefacts/

> **Agriculture Research Service: Sci4Kids**
> http://www.ars.usda.gov/is/kids/

> **Farm Service Agency: FSA Kids**
> http://www.fsa.usda.gov/FSA/kidsapp?area=home&subject=landing&topic=landing

U.S. Food and Drug Administration: Science and Our Food Supply
http://www.fda.gov/Food/ResourcesForYou/StudentsTeachers/ScienceandTheFoodSupply/default.htm

U.S. Working Group on the Food Crisis
http://usfoodcrisisgroup.org/

What's On My Food?
http://www.whatsonmyfood.org/

Why Hunger? Local and Regional Food Systems
http://www.whyhunger.org/programs/fslc/topics/local-a-regional-food-systems/faqs.html

Name: _____ ⠀⠀⠀ Date: _____

Chapter Eight: STEM Design Challenge

STEM Design Challenge Assessment

Objectives:

Student will be able to…

- Identify a problem.
- Brainstorm solutions for the problem.
- Select the best solution to the problem.
- Construct a model of the solution.
- Test the model.
- Evaluate the model.
- Redesign the model.
- Test the redesigned model.
- Retest the redesigned model.
- Communicate the results.

Assessment of Technological Design:

Directions: Fill in the chart with information about the plan/model you made.

Technological Design	Indicator	Evidence
Identified the problem	Problem was identified	
Identified a possible solution for the problem	List of brainstorming solutions was provided and one solution was identified to test	
Constructed a model and plan for the solution	Plan states specifically what materials to be used and steps explaining how the materials will be used	
Tested the model and plan	Plan and model were tested, data was recorded	
Evaluated the model/plan	Results of the data were analyzed, the plan/model was evaluated, problems with the plan were identified, solutions to the problems were identified	
Redesigned the model/plan	Plan was redesigned to solve the identified problems in the first plan/model, and the new plan was tested and evaluated	
Communicated the results	Presented plans and results to other students	

Name: _____ Date: _____

Science Inquiry Skills Assessment

Basic Skills	Indicators	Evidence that students demonstrated process skill
Classifying	Grouping, ordering, arranging, or distributing objects, events, or information into categories based on properties or criteria, according to some method or system.	
Observing	Using the senses (or extensions of the senses) to gather information about an object or event.	
Measuring	Using both standard and nonstandard measures or estimates to describe the dimensions of an object or event. Making quantitative observations.	
Inferring	Making an interpretation or conclusion based on reasoning to explain an observation.	
Communicating	Communicating ideas through speaking or writing. Students may share the results of investigations, collaborate on solving problems, and gather and interpret data both orally and in writing. Use graphs, charts, and diagrams to describe data.	
Predicting	Making a forecast of future events or conditions in the context of previous observations and experiences.	
Manipulating Materials	Handling or treating materials and equipment skillfully and effectively.	
Replicating	Performing acts that duplicate demonstrated symbols, patterns, or procedures.	
Using Numbers	Applying mathematical rules or formulas to calculate quantities or determine relationships from basic measurements.	
Developing Vocabulary	Specialized terminology and unique uses of common words in relation to a given topic need to be identified and given meaning.	
Questioning	Questions serve to focus inquiry, determine prior knowledge, and establish purposes or expectations for an investigation. An active search for information is promoted when questions are used.	
Using Cues	Key words and symbols convey significant meaning in messages. Organizational patterns facilitate comprehension of major ideas. Graphic features clarify textual information.	

Name:_____ Date:_____

Science Inquiry Skills Assessment

Integrated Skills	Indicators	Evidence that students demonstrated process skill
Creating Models	Displaying information by means of graphic illustrations or other multisensory representations.	
Formulating Hypotheses	Stating or constructing a statement that is testable about what is thought to be the expected outcome of an experiment (based on reasoning).	
Generalizing	Drawing general conclusions from particulars.	
Identifying & Controlling Variables	Recognizing the characteristics of objects or factors in events that are constant or change under different conditions and that can affect an experimental outcome, keeping most variables constant while manipulating only one (the independent) variable.	
Defining Operationally	Stating how to measure a variable in an experiment; defining a variable according to the actions or operations to be performed on or with it.	
Recording & Interpreting Data	Collecting bits of information about objects and events that illustrate a specific situation, organizing and analyzing data that have been obtained, and drawing conclusions from it by determining apparent patterns or relationships in the data.	
Making Decisions	Identifying alternatives and choosing a course of action from among alternatives after basing the judgment for the selection on justifiable reasons.	
Experimenting	Being able to conduct an experiment, including asking an appropriate question, stating a hypothesis, identifying and controlling variables, operationally defining those variables, designing a "fair" experiment, and interpreting the results of an experiment.	

Name: _____   Date: _____

Assessment of Technological Design

TEACHER NOTE: Use this rubric to assess the design of any of the models in the chapter activities.

Objectives:
Student will be able to…
- Identify a problem.
- Brainstorm ideas about how you might solve the problem.
- Draw a diagram of the model.
- Construct a model of the solution.
- Test the solution.
- Evaluate the solution.
- Identify how to make changes to improve the design.
- Make the needed changes.
- Retest and reevaluate the design.
- Share the results.

Assessment of Technological Design:

Directions: Fill in the chart with information about the plan/model you made.

Technological Design	Indicator	Evidence
Identified the problem	Problem was identified	
Identified a possible solution for the problem	List of brainstorming solutions was provided and one solution was identified to test	
Constructed a model and plan for the solution	Plan states specifically what materials to be used and steps explaining how the materials will be used	
Tested the model and plan	Plan and model were tested, data was recorded	
Evaluated the model/plan	Results of the data were analyzed and the plan/model was evaluated, problems with the plan were identified, solutions to the problems were identified	
Redesigned the model/plan	Plan was redesigned to solve the identified problems in the first plan/model, and the new plan was tested and evaluated	
Communicated the results	Presented plans and results to other students	

Science Process Skills

	Skills	Definition
B A S I C **P R O C E S S** **S K I L L S**	Classifying	Grouping, ordering, arranging, or distributing objects, events, or information into categories based on properties or criteria, according to some method or system.
	Observing	Using the senses (or extensions of the senses) to gather information about an object or event.
	Measuring	Using both standard and nonstandard measures or estimates to describe the dimensions of an object or event. Making quantitative observations.
	Inferring	Making an interpretation or conclusion based on reasoning to explain an observation.
	Communicating	Communicating ideas through speaking or writing. Students may share the results of investigations, collaborate on solving problems, and gather and interpret data both orally and in writing. Use graphs, charts, and diagrams to describe data.
	Predicting	Making a forecast of future events or conditions in the context of previous observations and experiences.
	Manipulating Materials	Handling or treating materials and equipment skillfully and effectively.
	Replicating	Performing acts that duplicate demonstrated symbols, patterns, or procedures.
	Using Numbers	Applying mathematical rules or formulas to calculate quantities or determine relationships from basic measurements.
	Developing Vocabulary	Specialized terminology and unique uses of common words in relation to a given topic need to be identified and given meaning.
	Questioning	Questions serve to focus inquiry, determine prior knowledge, and establish purposes or expectations for an investigation. An active search for information is promoted when questions are used.
	Using Cues	Key words and symbols convey significant meaning in messages. Organizational patterns facilitate comprehension of major ideas. Graphic features clarify textual information.

	Skills	Definition
I N T E G R A T E D **S K I L L S**	Creating Models	Displaying information by means of graphic illustrations or other multisensory representations.
	Formulating Hypotheses	Stating or constructing a statement that is testable about what is thought to be the expected outcome of an experiment (based on reasoning).
	Generalizing	Drawing general conclusions from particulars.
	Identifying & Controlling Variables	Recognizing the characteristics of objects or factors in events that are constant or change under different conditions and that can affect an experimental outcome, keeping most variables constant while manipulating only one (the independent) variable.
	Defining Operationally	Stating how to measure a variable in an experiment; defining a variable according to the actions or operations to be performed on or with it.
	Recording & Interpreting Data	Collecting bits of information about objects and events that illustrate a specific situation, organizing and analyzing data that have been obtained, and drawing conclusions from it by determining apparent patterns or relationships in the data.
	Making Decisions	Identifying alternatives and choosing a course of action from among alternatives after basing the judgment for the selection on justifiable reasons.
	Experimenting	Being able to conduct an experiment, including asking an appropriate question, stating a hypothesis, identifying and controlling variables, operationally defining those variables, designing a "fair" experiment, and interpreting the results of an experiment.

NSES Content Standards

Summary from the NRC (1996). *National Science Education Standards.* Washington, D.C.: National Academy Press.

Assumptions:
1. NSES Standards require changes throughout the system.
2. What students learn is influenced by how they are taught.
3. Actions of teachers are deeply influenced by their perceptions of science as an enterprise and as a subject to be taught and learned.
4. Student understanding is actively constructed through individual and social processes.
5. Actions of teachers are deeply influenced by their understanding of and relationships with students.

NSES Unifying Concepts and Processes:
Systems, Order, and Organization
Evidence, Models, and Explanations
Change, Constancy, and Measurement
Evolution and Equilibrium
Form and Function

NSES Content Standards:

Standard	Understanding	Indicators Grades 5–8 Students will be able to:
A. Science as Inquiry	Abilities to do scientific inquiry	Identify questions that can be answered through investigations.
		Plan and conduct a scientific investigation.
		Use appropriate tools and techniques to gather, analyze, and interpret data.
		Develop descriptions, explanations, predictions, and models using evidence.
		Think critically and logically to make the relationships between evidence and explanations.
		Recognize and analyze alternative explanations and predictions.
		Communicate scientific procedures and explanations.
		Use mathematics in all aspects of inquiry.
	Understanding scientific inquiry	Explain that different kinds of investigations are needed depending on the questions they are trying to answer.
		Explain that current scientific knowledge guides scientific investigations.
		Explain that mathematics is important to all aspects of inquiry.
		Explain that technology used to gather data increases accuracy and quantifies the results.
		Explain that scientists develop explanations from evidence from investigations and scientific knowledge.
		Explain that science advances through skepticism.
		Explain that scientific investigations may result in new ideas and investigations.

B. Physical Science	Properties and changes in properties of matter	Explain that substances have characteristic properties.
		Explain that substances react chemically in characteristic ways with other substances to form new substances (compounds) with different properties. Mass is conserved in chemical reactions.
		Explain that chemical elements do not break down during normal laboratory reactions. There are over 100 known elements that combine to form compounds.
	Motions and forces	Explain that motion can be described by its position, speed, and direction, and it can be measured.
		Explain an object in motion will move at a constant speed in a straight line until acted upon by another force.
		Explain if more than one force acts upon an object along a straight line, the forces either reinforce or cancel one another. Unbalanced forces will cause changes in the speed or direction of the motion.
	Transfer of energy	Explain that energy is a property of many substances and is transferred in many ways.
		Explain that heat moves in predictable ways, flowing from warmer to cooler areas until the temperature is equalized.
		Explain that light interacts with matter by transmission (including refraction), absorption, and scattering (including reflection).
		Explain electrical circuits are a means of transferring electrical energy.
		Explain that in most chemical and nuclear reactions energy is transferred into or out of a system.
		Explain that the sun is a major source of energy for changes on the earth's surface. The sun's energy arrives as light with a range of wavelengths—visible light, infrared, ultraviolet radiation.
C. Life Science	Structure and function of living systems	Explain that living systems demonstrate the complementary nature of function and structure. Levels of organization include cell, tissue, organ, systems, organism, and ecosystems.
		Explain that all organisms are composed of cells.
		Explain that cells carry on functions needed to sustain life, they grow and divide, take in nutrients, and get rid of wastes.
		Explain that specialized cells perform special functions. Groups of specialized cells make tissues; groups of specialized tissues form organs.
		Explain that humans have systems for digestion, respiration, reproduction, circulation, excretion, movement, control and coordination, and protection from diseases.
		Explain that disease is a breakdown in structures or functions of an organism.
	Reproduction and heredity	Explain that reproduction is a characteristic of all living systems.
		Explain in many species females produce eggs and males produce sperm. Egg and sperm unite to form a new organism. The new organism receives genetic information from the male and female.

		Explain that organisms require a set of instructions to specify its traits. Heredity is the passage of these instructions from one generation to another.
		Explain heredity information is contained in the genes in the chromosomes of each cell. A gene carries a single unit of information. Inherited traits are determined by the genes.
		Explain that characteristics of an organism are from the combination of traits. Some traits are inherited and some are from interactions with the environment.
	Regulation and behavior	Explain that all organisms must be able to obtain and use resources, grow, reproduce, and maintain stable internal conditions in a constantly changing environment.
		Explain that regulation of the internal environment involves sensing the environment and changing physiological activities to keep conditions within the range required to survive.
		Explain that behavior is one kind of response an organism makes to an internal or external stimulus.
		Explain that an organism's behavior evolves through adaptation to its environment.
	Populations and ecosystems	Describe a population as all individuals of a species that occur at a given place in a given time. An ecosystem is all populations and the physical factors with which they interact.
		Explain that populations can be categorized by the function they serve in an ecosystem—producers, consumers, decomposers. Food webs identify the relationships among organisms.
		Explain that the major source of energy in an ecosystem is sunlight.
		Explain that the number of organisms in an ecosystem depends on the resources available and abiotic factors.
	Diversity and adaptations of organisms	Explain that millions of species are alive today.
		Explain that biological evolution accounts for the diversity of species.
		Explain that extinction of a species occurs when an environment changes and it cannot adapt.
D. Earth Science	Structure of the earth system	Describe that the earth is layered with a lithosphere (crust), hot convecting mantle, and dense metal core.
		Explain that lithospheric (crustal) plates constantly move in response to movements in the mantle.
		Explain that landforms result from constructive and destructive forces.
		Describe the rock cycle as some of the changes in the solid earth.
		Describe soil as weathered rocks and decomposed organic matter.
		Explain that water covers the majority of the earth and it circulates through the crust, water, and atmosphere (water cycle).
		Explain that water is a solvent and dissolves minerals and gases as it passes through the water cycle.

		Explain that the atmosphere is a mixture of nitrogen, oxygen, and trace gases.
		Explain that clouds are formed by condensation.
		Explain that global patterns of atmospheric movement influence local weather.
		Explain that living organisms play many roles in the earth system.
	Earth's history	Explain that earth processes—erosion, movement of plates, and changes in the atmosphere—also occurred in the past.
		Explain that fossils provide evidence of the past.
	Earth in the solar system	Explain that the earth is the third planet from the sun in the solar system. The sun is an average star and is the central and largest body in the solar system.
		Explain most objects in the solar system are in regular predictable motion.
		Explain that gravity is the force that keeps planets in orbit around the sun. It holds everything on earth and controls the tides.
		Explain that the sun is the major source of energy for phenomena on the earth's surface.
E. Science and Technology	Abilities of technological design	Identify appropriate problems for technological design.
		Design a solution or product.
		Implement a proposed design.
		Evaluate completed designs or products.
		Communicate the process of technological design.
	Understanding of technological design	Explain that scientists propose explanations for the natural world. Engineers propose solutions relating to human needs, problems, and aspirations. Technological solutions are temporary; exist within nature so they can not contravene physical or biological principles; solutions may have side effects and costs, carry risks, and provide benefits.
		Explain many different people from many cultures have contributed to science and technology.
		Explain that science drives technology, and technology is essential to science.
		Explain that designed solutions are not perfect; they have trade-offs and risks.
		Explain that technological designs have constraints.
		Explain that technological solutions have intended benefits and unintended consequences.
F. Personal and Social Perspectives	Personal health	Regular exercise is important to maintain and improve health.
		Potential for accidents and hazards create a need for injury prevention.
		Use of tobacco increases the risk of illness.
		Alcohol and other drugs are often abused substances.
		Food provides energy and nutrients for growth and development.
		Sex drive is a natural human function that needs understanding.

		Natural environments may contain substances that are harmful to human beings.
	Populations, resources, and environments	Overpopulated environments will become degraded due to increased use of resources.
		Causes of environmental degradation and resources vary.
	Natural hazards	Internal and external processes of the earth cause natural hazards.
		Human activities can also cause natural hazards.
		Natural hazards can present personal and societal changes.
	Risks and benefits	Risk analysis considers the type of hazard and estimates the number of people that might be exposed and the number likely to suffer consequences.
		Risks are associated with natural hazards, chemical hazards, biological hazards, social hazards, and personal hazards.
		A systematic approach should be used for risk benefit analysis.
		Personal and social decisions are made based on perceptions of risks and benefits.
	Science and technology in society	Science influences society through its knowledge and world view.
		Societal challenges often inspire questions for scientific research and social priorities influence research through availability of funding.
		Technology influences society through its products and processes.
		Science and technology have advanced through different people in different cultures in different times in history.
		Scientists and engineers work in different settings.
		Scientists and engineers have ethical codes.
		Science cannot answer all questions and technology cannot solve all problems.
G. History and Nature of Science	Science as a human endeavor	People of diverse backgrounds engage in science, engineering, and related fields.
		Science requires different abilities.
	The nature of science	Scientists formulate and test explanations using observations, experiments, and theoretical and mathematic models.
		Scientists may have different opinions.
		Scientific inquiry includes evaluating results of investigations, experiments, observations, theoretical models, and explanations of other scientists.
	The history of science	Many individuals have contributed to the traditions of science.
		Science has been practiced by different individuals in different cultures.
		History shows how difficult it was for scientific innovators to break through the accepted ideas of their times.

Principles and Standards for School Mathematics 5–8 (NCTM)

National Council for Teachers of Mathematics. (2000). *Principles and Standards for School Mathematics.* Reston, VA: National Council for Teachers of Mathematics.

Standard	Indicators
Problem Solving	Use problem-solving approaches to investigate and understand mathematics.
	Formulate problems from situations.
	Develop and apply a variety of strategies to solve problems.
	Verify and interpret results.
	Generalize solutions and strategies to new problems.
	Acquire confidence in using mathematics.
Communication	Model situations using oral, written, concrete, pictorial, graphical, and algebraic methods.
	Reflect on and clarify their own thinking about mathematical ideas and situations.
	Develop common understandings of mathematical ideas.
	Use the skills of reading, listening, and viewing to interpret and evaluate mathematical ideas.
	Discuss mathematical ideas and make conjectures and arguments.
	Appreciate the value of mathematical notation.
Reasoning	Recognize and apply deductive and inductive reasoning.
	Use reasoning processes.
	Make and evaluate conjectures and arguments.
	Validate their own thinking.
	Appreciate the pervasive use and power of reasoning as a part of mathematics.
Mathematical Connections	See mathematics as an integrated whole.
	Explore problems and describe results using graphs; numbers; and physical, algebraic, and verbal models or representations.
	Use a mathematical idea to further their understanding of mathematics.
	Apply mathematical thinking and modeling to solve problems.
	Value the role of mathematics in our culture and society.
Number and Number Relationships	Use numbers in a variety of forms.
	Develop number sense.
	Use ratios, proportions, and percents in a variety of situations.
	Investigate relationships among fractions, decimals, and percents.
	Represent numerical relationships on graphs.
Number Systems/ Number Theory	Understand the need for numbers beyond whole numbers.
	Develop and use order relations.
	Extend understanding of whole number operations to fractions, decimals, integers, and rational numbers.
	Understand how basic arithmetic operations are related to one another.
	Develop and apply number theory in real-world problems.
Computation and Estimation	Compute with whole numbers, fractions, decimals, integers, and rational numbers.
	Develop, analyze, and explain methods for computation and estimation.
	Select and use appropriate methods for computing.
	Use computation, estimation, and proportions to solve problems.
	Use estimation to check reasonableness.

Patterns and Functions	Describe, extend, analyze, and create patterns.
	Describe and represent relationships with tables, graphs, and rules.
	Analyze functional relationships to explain how a change in one changes another.
	Use patterns and functions to represent and solve problems.
Algebra	Understand variables, expressions, and equations.
	Represent situations and number patterns with tables, graphs, verbal rules, and equations and their interrelationships.
	Analyze tables and graphs to identify properties and relationships.
	Develop confidence in solving linear equations.
	Investigate inequalities and nonlinear equations.
	Apply algebraic methods to solve problems.
Statistics	Systematically collect, organize, and describe data.
	Construct, read, and interpret tables, graphs, and charts.
	Make inferences and arguments based on data analysis.
	Evaluate arguments based on data analysis.
	Develop appreciation for statistical methods for decision making.
Probability	Model situations by devising and carrying out experiments or simulations to determine probabilities.
	Model situations by constructing a sample space to determine probabilities.
	Appreciate the power of using a probability model.
	Make predictions based on experimental or theoretical probabilities.
	Develop an appreciation for the use of probability in the real world.
Geometry	Identify, describe, compare, and classify geometric figures.
	Visualize and represent geometric figures.
	Explore transformations of geometric figures.
	Represent and solve problems using geometric figures.
	Understand and apply geometric properties and relationships.
	Develop appreciation of geometry as a means of describing the physical world.
Measurement	Extend understanding of processes of measurement.
	Estimate, make, and use measurement to describe and compare phenomena.
	Select appropriate units and tools.
	Understand the structure and use of measurement systems.
	Understand perimeter, area, volume, angle measurement, capacity, weight, and mass.
	Develop concepts of rate and other derived and indirect measurements.
	Develop formulas and procedures for determining measures to solve problems.

ITEA Standards for Technological Literacy

Adapted from: International Technology Education Association (2007) *Standards for Technological Literacy*. Reston, VA: International Technology Education Association. URL: www.iteaconnect.org

Standards for Technological Literacy:

Goal	Standard	Grades 6–8 Indicators
Students will develop an understanding of the Nature of Technology.	Students will develop understanding of:	Students will be able to:
	1. Characteristics and scope of technology	Explain that new products and systems can be developed to solve problems or help do things that could not be done without the help of technology.
		Explain that technology is a human activity and is the result of individual and collective needs and the ability to be creative.
		Explain that technology is closely linked to creativity which has resulted in innovation.
		Explain that corporations can create a demand for a product by bringing it onto a market and advertising it.
	2. Core concepts of technology	Describe that technological systems include input, processes, output, and feedback.
		Explain that technological systems can be connected to one another.
		Explain that malfunctions of any part of a system may affect the function and quality of the system.
		Describe that trade-off is a decision process recognizing the need for careful compromises among competing factors.
		Explain that different technologies involve different sets of processes.
		Describe maintenance as a process of inspecting and servicing a product or system on a regular basis so that it continues to function properly, to extend life or upgrade its capability.
		Describe that controls are mechanisms or particular steps performed using information about the system that causes systems to change.
	3. Relationships among technologies and the connections between technology and other fields	Explain that technological systems often interact with one another.
		Explain that a product, system, or environment developed for one setting may be applied to another setting.
		Explain that knowledge from other fields has a direct effect on the development of technology.
Students will develop an understanding of Technology and Society.	Students will develop understanding of:	Students will be able to:
	4. Cultural, social, economic, and political effects of technology	Explain that the use of technology affects humans in various ways—safety, comfort, choices, and attitudes about technology's development and use.

		Explain that technology is neither good nor bad, but the decisions about the use of it can result in desirable or undesirable consequences.
		Explain that development and use of technology poses ethical questions.
		Explain that economic, political, and cultural issues are influenced by the development and use of technology.
	5. Effects of technology on the environment	Explain the management of waste produced by technological systems is a societal issue.
		Explain that technologies can be used to repair damage caused by natural disasters and break down wastes.
		Explain that the development and use of technologies put environmental and economic concerns in competition with one another.
	6. Role of society in the development and use of technology	Explain that throughout history new technologies have resulted from demands, values, and interests of individuals, businesses, industries, and societies.
		Explain that the use of inventions and innovations has led to changes in society and creation of new needs and wants.
		Explain that social and cultural priorities and values are reflected in the technological devices.
		Explain that meeting social expectations is the driving force behind the acceptance and use of products and systems.
	7. The Influence of technology on history	Explain that many inventions and innovations have evolved by using a methodical process of tests and refinements.
		Explain the specialization of function has been at the head of many technological improvements.
		Explain that the design and construction of structures for service or convenience have evolved from the development of techniques for measurement, controlling systems, and understanding of spatial relationships.
		Explain that in the past, an invention or innovation was not usually developed with the knowledge of science.
Students will develop an understanding of Design	Students will develop an understanding of:	Students will be able to:
	8. The attributes of design	Describe design as a creative process that leads to useful products and systems.
		Explain there is no perfect design.
		Explain that the requirements for a design are made up of criteria and constraints.
	9. Engineering design	Explain that design involves a set of steps that can be performed in different sequences and repeated as needed.
		Describe brainstorming—a group problem solving process in which each person presents their ideas in an open forum.
		Explain that modeling, testing, evaluating, and modifying are used to transform ideas into practical solutions.
	10. The role of troubleshooting, research and development, invention and innovation, and experimentation in problem solving	Describe troubleshooting as a way of identifying the cause of a malfunction in a technological system.
		Explain that invention is a process of turning ideas and imagination into devices and systems. Explain innovation is the process of modifying an existing product to improve it.

		Explain that some technological problems are best solved through science experimentations.
Students will develop Abilities for a Technological World.	Students will be able to:	Students will be able to:
	11. Apply the design process	Apply a design process to solve a problem.
		Make two- and three-dimensional representations of the design solution.
		Test and evaluate the design related to pre-established criteria.
		Make a product or system and document the solution.
	12. Use and maintain technological products and systems	Use information provided to see and understand how things work.
		Use tools, materials, and machines safely to diagnose, adjust, and repair systems.
		Use computers and calculators in various applications.
		Operate and maintain systems in order to achieve a given purpose.
	13. Assess the impact of products and systems	Design and use instruments to gather data.
		Use data collected to analyze and interpret trends in order to identify the positive or negative effects of a technology.
		Identify trends and monitor potential consequences of technological development.
		Interpret and evaluate the accuracy of the information obtained, and determine if it is useful.
Students will develop an understanding of the Designed World.	Students will develop an understanding of and be able to select and use the following:	Students will be able to:
	14. Medical technologies	Explain advances in medical technologies are used to improve health care.
		Explain that sanitation processes used in the disposal of medical products help protect people from harmful organisms and disease and shape the ethics of medical safety.
		Explain that vaccines developed for immunizations require specialized technologies to support environments in which sufficient amounts of vaccines are produced.
		Describe that genetic engineering involves modifying the structure of DNA to produce novel genetic makeups.
	15. Agricultural and related biotechnologies	Explain that technological advances in agriculture affect the time and number of people required to produce food for large populations.
		Explain that a wide range of specialized equipment and practices are used to improve the production of food, fiber, fuel, and other products and in the care of animals.
		Describe that biotechnology applies the principles of biology to create products or processes.
		Explain that artificial ecosystems are human made environments that are designed to replicate a natural environment.
		Describe that the development of refrigeration, freezing, dehydration, preservation, and irradiation provide long-term storage of food and reduce the health risks of tainted food.

	16. Energy and power technologies	Explain that energy has the capacity to do work.
		Explain that energy can be used to do work using many processes.
		Explain that power is the rate at which energy is converted from one form to another, or transferred from one place to another, or the rate at which work is done.
		Describe that power systems are used to drive and provide propulsion to other products and systems.
		Explain that much of the energy used in our environment is not used efficiently.
	17. Information and communication technologies	Explain that information and communication allow information to be transferred from human to human, human to machine, and machine to human.
		Describe communication systems are made up of a source, encoder, transmitter, receiver, decoder, and destination.
		Describe that the design of a message is influenced by: intended audience, medium, purpose, and nature of the message.
		Explain the use of symbols, measurements, and drawings promotes clear communication by providing a common language to express ideas.
	18. Transportation technologies	Describe that transporting people and goods involves a combination of individuals or vehicles.
		Explain that transportation vehicles are made up of subsystems that must function together.
	19. Manufacturing technologies	Explain that manufacturing systems use mechanical processes that change the form of materials.
		Explain that manufactured goods can be durable or nondurable.
		Describe that the manufacturing process includes: designing, development, making, and servicing products and systems.
		Explain that chemical technologies are used to modify or alter chemical substances.
		Explain that materials must be located before they can be extracted from the earth.
		Explain that marketing involves informing the public about it as well as assisting in selling and distribution.
	20. Construction technologies	Explain that the selection of designs for structures is based on: building laws, codes, style, convenience, cost, climate, and function.
		Explain that structures rest on a foundation.
		Explain that some structures are temporary and some are permanent.
		Explain that buildings contain subsystems.

Assessment Answer Keys

Chapter One: Food Production Issues (p. 15)

1–3. Answers will vary.

Chapter Two: Biologically Productive Land and Water (p. 32–33)

1. c   2. e   3. f   4. a
5. b
6. Answers will vary.   7. 72% water
8. 4%   9. 28% land
10. 19% is biologically productive
11. Answers will vary.

Chapter Three: Food Systems (p. 43–44)

1. c   2. i   3. e   4. b
5. d   6. f   7. g   8. a
9. h
10–12. Answers will vary.
13. Plants use the sun's energy to make food for all consumers. Plants are the only producers.
14. Plants use the sun's energy to make food, and the energy is passed down through the food chains to the consumers.

Chapter Four: Food and Energy (p. 53–54)

1. i   2. c   3. h   4. a
5. b   6. d   7. e   8. g
9. f
10. Food provides the energy and nutrients needed for survival. Energy is released from food when it is metabolized.
11. At each level, only 10% of the energy is passed on to the next consumer. Ninety percent is lost as heat energy and waste.
12. If people eat meat, they receive less energy. Plants get 10% of the sun's energy, while the next level of consumer gets 1% of the energy, and the next level gets only 0.1%.
13. Answers will vary.
14. You would become overweight.
15. Diet and exercise are needed.

Chapter Five: Farming (p. 66–67)

1. n   2. k   3. i   4. e
5. d   6. b   7. j   8. m
9. l   10. g   11. f   12. a
13. h   14. c
15. There has been an increase in population and a need for more food. New science, technology, and engineering have been developed to meet that need.
16. Answers will vary. Possible answers are tractors, genetic engineering, etc.
17. More food can be produced on the same amount of land, but runoff can lead to soil and water contamination.
18. Answers will vary.

Chapter Six: Hydroponics (p. 81–82)

1. g   2. b   3. a   4. e
5. f   6. d   7. c
8. Answers will vary depending on which system is described.
9. Students should describe water culture, aeroponics, and aggregate systems.
10. Answers will vary but should include it uses less land, uses nutrients efficiently, is expensive, and is a good environment for *salmonella* to grow.

Chapter Seven: Food Processing and Preservation (p. 92–93)

1. e   2. d   3. a   4. c
5. b   6. g   7. h   8. f
9. Answers will vary but could include to be able to store foods longer, transport foods, convenience, and reduce the possible contamination of food.
10. Drying, freezing, canning, curing, etc.
11. Answers will vary but could include pollution from use of fossil fuels, wastes, contamination of the food supply, etc.

Chapter Eight: Design Challenge (p. 101)

See rubric.

References

Books:

Ansberry, Karen and Emily Morgan. *Picture Perfect Science Lessons*. Alexandria, VA: National Science Teacher's Association. 2010.

Baines, John. *Food and Farming*. New York: Smart Apple Media. 2008.

Barnett, Anne and Hazel King. *Food Processing*. New York: Heinemann Library. 2008.

Bowden, Rob. *Food and Water*. Cambridge, MA: Smart Apple Media. 2009.

Burstein, John. *Energy In, Energy Out: Food as Fuel*. New York: Crabtree Publishing. 2008.

Canizares, Susan and Pamela Chanko. *Water*. New York, NY: Scholastic Inc. 1998

Carlson, Laurie. *Green Thumbs: A Kid's Activity Guide to Indoor and Outdoor Gardening*. Chicago: Chicago Review Press. 2010.

Carson, Rachel. *Silent Spring: 40th Anniversary Edition*. New York, NY: Mariner Books. 2002.

Casper, Julie Kerr. *Agriculture: The Food We Grow and Animals We Raise*. New York: Chelsea House Publications. 2007.

Charles, Daniel. *Lords of the Harvest: Biotech, Big Money, and the Future of Food*. Cambridge, MA: Perseus Publishing. 2002.

Cole, Jenna. *The Magic School Bus: At the Waterworks*. New York, NY: Scholastic. 1986.

D'Aluisio, Faith and Peter Menzel. *What the World Eats*. Berkeley, CA: Tricycle Press. 2008.

Featherstone, Jane. *Earth Alert!: Farming*. New York: Hodder Wayland. 2001.

Genetic Modification of Food. New York: Heinemann Library. 2005.

Goodman, Polly. *Earth in Danger: Farming*. New York: Hodder Wayland. 2005.

Grant, Tim and Gail Littlejohn. *Teaching Green: The Middle Years*. Ontario, Canada: New Society Publishers. 2004.

Gray, Susan Heinrichs. *Food Webs: Interconnecting Food Chains*. New York: Compass Points Books. 2008

Heinz, Brian. *Butternut Hollow Pond*. Minneapolis, MN: Millbrook Press. 2005.

Holt-Gimenéz, Eric. *Food Rebellions: Crisis and the Hunger for Justice*. Oakland, CA: Food First Books. 2009.

Hooper, Meredith. *The Drop in My Drink: The Story of Water on Our Planet*. London: Frances Lincoln Children's Books. 1998.

Hooks, Gwendolyn. *Makers and Takers: Studying Food Webs in the Ocean*. Florida: Rourke Pub. 2008.

Jakab, Cheryl. *Ecological Footprints*. New York: Benchmark Books. 2010.

Jango-Cohen, Judith. *The History of Food*. Connecticut: Twenty-First Century Books. 2005.

Kalman, Bobbie. *Food Chains and You*. New York: Crabtree Publishing. 2004

Karas, G. Brian. *On Earth*. New York: Puffin. 2005.

Kent, Kay, Barbara Aston, Myrna Mitchell, Barbara Ann Novelli, and Michelle Pauls. *Sensational Springtime*. Fresno, CA: AIMS Education Foundation. 2007.

Kerr, Jim. *Food: Ethical Debates on What We Eat*. Cambridge, MA: Smart Apple Media. 2008.

Kimbrell, Andrew. *Fatal Harvest: The Tragedy of Industrial Agriculture*. Washington, D.C.: Island Press. 2002.

Lauber, Patricia. *Who Eats What? Food Chains and Webs*. New York, NY: Harper Collins. 1994.

Lawrence Hall of Science. *FOSS Science Stories: Water*. Nashua, NH: Delta Education. 2003.

Lindob, David L. *Soil! Get the Inside Scoop*. Madison, WI: American Society of Agronomy. 2008.

Mason, Paul. *Food*. New York: Heinemann-Raintree. 2005.

McGinty, Alice B. *Carnivores in the Food Chain*. New York: PowerKid Press. 2002

Menzel, Peter. *What I Eat: Around the World in 80 Diets*. Napa, CA: Material World. 2010.

Montgomery, David R. *Dirt: The Erosion of Civilization*. Berkeley, CA: University of California Press. 2008.

Murray, Julie. *Cocoa Bean to Chocolate*. Edina, MA: Buddy Books. 2006.

Pollan, Michael. *The Omnivore's Dilemma for Kids: The Secrets Behind What You Eat*. New York: Dial. 2009.

Project WILD. Houston, TX: Council for Environmental Education. 2007.

Project WILD Aquatic. Houston, TX: Council for Environmental Education. 2005

Rapp, Valerie. *Protecting Earth's Land*. New York: Learner Publications. 2008.

Riley, Peter. *Food Chains*. Danbury, CT: First Avenue Editions. 2010.

Rodger, Ellen. *Reduce Your Footprint: Farming, Cooking, and Eating for a Healthy Planet*. New York: Crabtree Publishing. 2010.

Rooney, Anne. *Feeding the World*. Cambridge, MA: Smart Apple Media. 2009.

Slade, Suzanne. *What Do You Know About Food Chains and Food Webs?* New York: PowerKid Press. 2008

Smith, Angela. *The Effects of Farming*. New York: Franklin Watts, LTD. 2006.

Smith, Jeffrey M. *Seeds of Deception: Exposing Industry and Government Lies About the Safety of the Genetically Engineered Foods You're Eating*. Fairfield, IA: Yes! Books. 2003.

Solway, Andrew. *Food Chains and Webs*. Florida: Rourke Pub. 2009.

Steingraber, Sandra. *Living Downstream*. Cambridge MA: DaCapo Press. 2010.

Tudge, Colin. *Food for the Future*. New York: Dorling Kindersley Publishing, Inc. 2002.

VanCleave, Janice. *Food and Nutrition for Every Kid*. New York: Wiley. 1999.

Wilkes, Angela. *A Farm Through Time: The History of a Farm From Medieval Times to the Present Day*. New York: Dorling Kindersley Publishing, Inc. 2001.

Wilson, Michael R. *Hunger: Food Insecurity in America*. New York: Rosen Publishing Group. 2009.

Wolny, Philip. *Food Supply Collapse*. New York: Rosen Publishing Group. 2010.

Websites:

4-H
http://www.4-h.org/

The Accidental Scientist: Science of Cooking
http://www.exploratorium.edu/cooking/index.html

Adventures With Bobbie Bigfoot
http://www.kidsfootprint.org/

Agriculture and Food Systems
http://www.sustainable.org/economy/
agriculture-a-food-systems

Agriculture in the Classroom: Kids' Zone
http://www.agclassroom.org/kids/index.htm

Agropolis Museum: Food and Agricultures of the World
http://museum.agropolis.fr/english/default.htm

Alabama Cooperative Extension System: Hydroponics for Home Gardeners
http://www.aces.edu/pubs/docs/A/ANR-1151/

Alternative Energy Base: Hydroponics in Commercial Food Production
http://www.alternativeenergybase.com/Article/
Hydroponics-in-commercial-food-production/787

American Community Gardening Association
www.communitygarden.org

Aquaponic Gardening: What is Aquaponics?
http://aquaponicscommunity.com/page/
what-is-aquaponics

Are We Eating Our Way Into a Crisis?
http://myecoproject.org/get-involved/
organic-living/

ATTRA: Aquaponics – Integration of Hydroponics With Aquaculture
http://www.aces.edu/dept/fisheries/education/
documents/Horticulturesystemsguide.pdf

Basic Hydroponic Systems
http://www.simplyhydro.com/system.htm

BBC: GCSE Bitesize: Food Chains
http://www.bbc.co.uk/schools/gcsebitesize/science/
add_aqa/foodchains/foodchains1.shtml

BBC and Nutrition
http://www.bbc.co.uk/health/treatments/
healthy_living/nutrition/index.shtml

BBC: Sea Life: Blue Planet Challenge
http://www.bbc.co.uk/nature/blueplanet/webs/flash/
main_game.shtml

Braums Dairy: Just For Kids
http://www.braums.com/JustKids/AllAboutCows2.asp

Brooklyn Botanic Gardens: Composting Basics
http://www.bbg.org/gardening/article/composting_
basics/

Bureau of Labor Statistics: Occupational Outlook Handbook, 2010-11 Edition: Agricultural and Food Scientists
http://www.bls.gov/oco/ocos046.htm

Care 2 Make a Difference?
http://www.care2.com/channels/ecoinfo/kids

Center for Ecoliteracy
www.ecoliteracy.org

Center for Food Safety
http://truefoodnow.org/

Chain Reaction: Build a Food Chain
http://www.ecokids.ca./pub/eco_info/topics/frogs/
chain_reation/index.cfm

Chipper Woods Bird Sanctuary: Owls and Owl Pellets
http://www.wbu.com/chipperwoods/photos/owls.htm

City Farmer
www.cityfarmer.info

Cool Foods Campaign
http://coolfoodscampaign.org/

Cornell University: Agricultural Outreach and Education
http://agout.cals.cornell.edu/

> **Discovering the Food Systems**
> http://www.hort.cornell.edu/department/faculty/
> eames/foodsys/index.html
>
> **Milk Processing**
> http://www.milkfacts.info/MilkProcessing/
> MilkProcessingPage.htm
>
> **A Primer on Community Food Systems**
> http://www.hort.cornell.edu/department/
> faculty/eames/foodsys/primer.html

Dietary Recommendations for Healthy Children
http://www.heart.org/HEARTORG/GettingHealthy/
Dietary-Recommendations-for-Healthy-Children_UCM_
303886-Article.jsp

Discovery Health: How Calories Work
http://health.howstuffworks.com/wellness/
diet-fitness/weight-loss/calorie.htm

Earth Day Network Footprint Calculator
http://earthday.net/footprint/flash.html

Ecological Footprint Calculator
http://www.myfootprint.org/

Enchanted Learning: Food Chains and Food Webs
http://www.enchantedlearning.com/subjects/foodchain/

Encyclopædia Britannica: Fats and Oils Processing
http://www.britannica.com/EBchecked/topic/202405/
fat-processing

> **Meat Processing**
> http://www.britannica.com/EBchecked/topic/
> 371756/meat-processing

Food and Energy and Strategies for Sustainable Development
http://www.unu.edu/unupress/unupbooks/80757e/
80757e00.htm

Food First
http://www.foodfirst.org/

The Food Guide Pyramid
http://kidshealth.org/kid/stay_healthy/food/pyramid.html

Food Processing.com
http://www.foodprocessing.com/

A Historical Timeline of Food Processing
http://www.foodprocessing.com/articles/2010/
anniversary.html

Food Safety: A 3-Part Series
http://www.foodprocessing.com/articles/2010/
foodsafety.html

> **Happy 200th Birthday, Can!**
> http://www.foodprocessing.com/articles/2010/
> octobertoops.html

Food Processing Technology
http://www.foodprocessing-technology.com/

Food Security and Dietary Health
http://www.cohabnet.org/en_issue2.htm

The Food Trust
http://www.thefoodtrust.org

Gardening–Tips–Idea.com: Learning about Hydroponics for Kids
http://www.gardening–tips–idea.com/
HydroponicsforKids.html

Geography4Kids.com: Another Link in the Food Chain
http://www.geography4kids.com/files/
land_foodchain.htm

Global Footprint Network
http://www.footprintnetwork.org/

Gould League: Build Your Own Food Webs
http://www.gould.edu.au/foodwebs/kids_web.htm

Green Schools
http://www.greenschools.net/form.pp?modin=53

Grodan: Hydroponics in Education
http://www.grodan101.com/sw63114.php

> **Hydroponic Experiments for Kids**
> http://www.grodan101.com/sw63175.php

Growell Hydroponics
http://www.growell.co.uk/pr/60/Deep-Water-Culture-
It-s-all-about-the-bubbles-.html

Growing a Nation: A History of American Agriculture
http://www.agclassroom.org/gan/timeline/index.htm

Heifer Project
www.heifer.org

How Cooking Oils Are Made
http://www.madehow.com/Volume-1/Cooking-Oil.html

How Stuff Works?: Hydroponics
http://tlc.howstuffworks.com/home/hydroponics.htm

Hydrofarm: Introduction to Hydroponics
http://www.hydrofarm.com/kb_introtohydro.php

Hydro for Hunger
http://www.hydroforhunger.org

Hydroponics Classroom: Hydroponics 101
http://www.hydroponicsclassroom.com/
hydroponics_101.html

Hydroponics Simplified: Getting Your Garden Growing
http://www.hydroponics-simplified.com/
hydroponics-seeds.html

ICLEI Global: Local Governments for Sustainability
http://www.iclei.org/

Identify the Food Chains
http://www.cas.psu.edu/DOCS/WEBCOURSE/
WETLAND/WED1/identify.html

Important Food Basics: Energy
http://www.healthyeatingclub.org/info/books-phds/
books/foodfacts/html/data/data2a.html

INPHO: Cereal Processing
http://www.fao.org/inpho/content/fpt/CEREALS/
prbread.htm

Institute of Science in Society: FAO Promotes Organic Agriculture
http://www.i-sis.org.uk/FAOPromotesOrganic
Agriculture.php

Institute of Simplified Hydroponics
http://www.carbon.org

International Center for Food Industry Excellence
http://www.icfie.com/

International Society for Horticulture Science
http://www.ishs.org

Iowa State University Extension: Food Irradiation – What is it?
http://www.extension.iastate.edu/foodsafety/irradiation/
info/MilkProcessing/

Kids Can Make a Difference
http://www.kidscanmakeadifference.org

Kids Gardening
http://www.kidsgardening.com

> **Exploring Classroom Hydroponics**
> http://www.kidsgardening.com/
> HYDROPONICSGUIDE/hydro1-1-intro.asp

Kids' Guide to Food: Food Processing
http://tiki.oneworld.net/food/food5.html

KidsHealth: Learning About Calories
http://kidshealth.org/kid/stay_healthy/food/calorie.html

What's a Vegetarian?
http://kidshealth.org/kid/stay_healthy/food/
vegetarian.html

Kidwings
http://www.kidwings.com/owlpellets/flash/v4/index.htm

The Life and Legacy of Rachel Carson
http://www.rachelcarson.org/

Louis Pasteur
http://www.accessexcellence.org/RC/AB/BC/
Louis_Pasteur.php

Mark Winne: High Food Prices: Just Another Bad Day in the Food Line
http://www.markwinne.com/52/

Merck: Food Additives and Contaminants
http://www.merck.com/mmhe/sec12/ch152/ch152e.html

MREInfo.com: MREs (Meals, Ready-to-Eat)
http://www.mreinfo.com/us/mre/mres.html

National Center for Home Food Preservation
http://www.uga.edu/nchfp/

National Heart Lung and Blood Institute: Balance Food and Activity
http://www.nhlbi.nih.gov/health/public/heart/obesity/
wecan/healthy-weight-basics/balance.htm

Natural Resources Defense Council: The Green Squad
http://www.nrdc.org/greensquad/intro/intro_1.asp

> **The Story of Silent Spring**
> http://www.nrdc.org/health/pesticides/hcarson.asp

The Natural Step
http://www.naturalstep.org/

Newagehydro
http://www.newagehydro.com/shop/faq.php

The New York Times: The Spotless Garden
http://www.nytimes.com/2010/20/18/garden/
18aqua.html?_r=1

Ocean Arks International
http://www.oceanarks.org/

> **Ecological Food Production**
> http://www.oceanarks.org/Ecological_Food_
> Production.php

Organic Consumers Association: Why Industrialized & Globalized Farm and Food Production is Not Sustainable
http://www.organicconsumers.org/BTC/
meacher091905.cfm

The Owl Pages: Digestion in Owls
http://www.owlpages.com/articles.php?
section=owl+physiology&title=Digestion

PBS: The Living Edens: Feed Me
http://www.pbs.org/edens/etosha/feedme.htm

Progressive Gardening: Soil Free Hydroponic Gardening
http://www.progressivegardening.com/
soilfreehydroponicgardening.html

Rodale Institute: Kids & Families
www.rodaleinstitute.org/organic_kids

Rutgers University: From Farm to Fork
http://njaes.rutgers.edu/health/farmtofork.asp

From Our Farm: Teaching Kids About Food, Nutrition, and the Farm
http://gloucester.njaes.rutgers.edu/fchs/
fromourfarms.html

School Carbon Footprint Calculator
http://www.dott07.com/flash/dott_024.htm

Science & Health Education Partnership: Measuring Calories in Food
http://www.seplessons.org/node/349

The Science of Energy Balance: Calorie Intake and Physical Activity
http://science.education.nih.gov/supplements/nih4/
energy/default.htm

Science Tech
http://www.techno-preneur.net/information-desk/
sciencetech-magazine/2007/jan07/Hydroponics.pdf

Stealth Hydroponics
http://www.stealthhydroponics.com

Sustainable Food Center
http://www.sustainablefoodcenter.org/

Sustainable Food Systems
http://www.sustainablefoodsystems.com

Sustainweb: 7 Principles of Sustainable Food
http://www.sustainweb.org/sustainablefood/

Thinkquest: Apples to Zucchinis: The Story of Food
http://library.thinkquest.org/C001722/farming.html

TLC Cooking: How Food Works
http://recipes.howstuffworks.com/food.htm

TLC Cooking: What are Calories?
http://recipes.howstuffworks.com/question670.htm

United Nations: Food and Agricultural Organization
http://www.fao.org/

22 Countries in Protracted Crisis
www.fao.org/news/sroy/en/item/46114/icode/

Dramatic Changes in Global Meat Production Could Increase Risk of Human Diseases
http://www.un.org/apps/news/story.asp?NewsID=
23824&Cr=livestock&Cr1=

U.S. Department of Agriculture
http://www.usda.gov/

Agriculture Research Service: Sci4Kids
http://www.ars.usda.gov/is/kids/

Economic Research Service: State Fact Sheets
http://www.ers.usda.gov/statefacts/

Economic Research Service: Land Use, Value, and Management
http://www.ers.usda.gov/Briefing/LandUse/
measuringurbanchapter.htm

Farm Service Agency: FSA Kids
http://www.fsa.usda.gov/FSA/kidsapp?area=
home&subject=landing&topic=landing

U.S. Food and Drug Administration
http://www.fda.gov/NewsEvents/Testimony/
ucm096475.htm

Science and Our Food Supply
http://www.fda.gov/Food/ResourcesForYou/Students
Teachers/ScienceandTheFoodSupply/default.htm

U.S. Working Group on the Food Crisis
http://usfoodcrisisgroup.org/

Wisconsin Fast Plants
http://www.fastplants.org/

What Does 200 Calories Look Like?
www.wisegeek.com/what-does-200-calories-look-like

What's On My Food?
http://www.whatsonmyfood.org/

Why Hunger? Local and Regional Food Systems
http://www.whyhunger.org/programs/fslc/
topics/local-a-regional-food-systems/faqs.html

World Food Programme: Food Quality Control
http://foodquality.wfp.org/FoodNutritionalQuality/
Energy/tabid/114/Default.aspx?PageContentmode=1

World Owl Trust
http://www.owls.org/Information/pellets.htm

Zerofootprint KidsCalculator
http://www.zerofootprintkids.com/kids_home.aspx

Video Resources

Food, Inc.
http://www.foodincmovie.com/

The Future of Food
http://www.thefutureoffood.com/